JOHN OF THE CROSS-- THE SPIRITUAL CANTICLE:

THE ENCOUNTER OF TWO LOVERS

An Introduction to the Book of the Spiritual Canticle by John of the Cross

LEONARD DOOHAN

ABBREVIATIONS OF THE WORKS

A = Ascent of Mount Carmel
N = Dark Night
C= Spiritual Canticle
F = Living Flame
P = Poetry
S = Sayings of Light and Love
Pr = Precautions
L = Letters

The Author

Dr. Leonard Doohan is Professor Emeritus at Gonzaga University where he was a professor of religious studies for 27 years and Dean of the Graduate School for 13 years. He has written 18 books and 160 articles and has given over 350 workshops throughout the US, Canada, Europe, Australia, New Zealand, and the Far East. Leonard's recent books include *Spiritual Leadership: the Quest for Integrity*, published by Paulist Press in 2007, *Enjoying Retirement: Living Life to the Fullest*, published by Paulist Press in 2010, *Courageous Hope: The Call of Leadership*, published by Paulist Press in 2011, and The *One Thing Necessary: The Transforming Power of Christian Love*, published by ACTA Publications in 2012.

Dr. Doohan has given courses and workshops on John of the Cross all over the world and his published tapes and cds have been used throughout the English speaking countries. Leonard's first book on John of the Cross, *The Contemporary Challenge of John of the Cross*, was published in 1995.

This current book is the third in a new series that explores the major works of John of the Cross for the non-specialist, presenting all the needed background to appreciate this wonderful spiritual writer.

Other books on John of the Cross by Leonard Doohan.

The Contemporary Challenge of John of the Cross
(ICS Publications)

John of the Cross: Your spiritual guide

The Dark Night is Our Only Light: A study of the
book of the *Dark Night* by John of the Cross

The Spiritual Canticle: The Encounter of Two Lovers.
An introduction to the book of the *Spiritual
Canticle* by John of the Cross

The Living Flame of Love (Due in 2014).

Table of contents

INTRODUCTION

The poem of the *Spiritual Canticle* is John of the Cross' longest poem, probably his favorite, and the one that gives us a glimpse into his own spiritual journey while in prison in Toledo. He wrote thirty-one of the forty stanzas during his time in the Toledan prison with its oppression and darkness. Yet this poem speaks to us of liberation, beauty, and loving union. He gave more attention to the commentary than to any of his other works, and it is clearly one of the most important spiritual writings in the history of spirituality.

This book is an introduction to John's masterpiece, if you wish, a study-guide. It gives the reader a thorough preparation for reading the *Spiritual Canticle*. Chapter one presents John's life and ministry, focusing on his life of love and his work as a poet of divine and human love. It then reflects on the book itself in chapter two—its history, dynamic outline, language of love, and some issues to be aware of when reading it. John's disciples called this work the *Spiritual Canticle* because of its close links to the *Song of Songs*, and so in chapter three we will examine the relationship, their common themes, and John's use of the *Song of Songs* in his *Spiritual Canticle*. Chapter four presents an abbreviation of John's *Spiritual Canticle*, following his four clearly established sections: I. An anxious search for one's lover; II. Encounter with one's lover in spiritual betrothal; III. The experience of union in spiritual marriage; and IV: The desire for fullness of union in eternity.

The book then moves in chapter five to study the dynamism of the spiritual life in the *Spiritual Canticle*, identifying the various stages through which the soul passes in this journey; a stage of purification followed by a period of illumination, then the two parts in the unitive stage of spiritual growth—spiritual betrothal and spiritual marriage. We then set aside two chapters, six and seven, to reflect on the key concepts in the *Spiritual Canticle*, those that refer to God in chapter six and those that refer to the bride in chapter seven. These great themes weave their way through this wonderful work with their profound spiritual challenges. John tells us how God is hidden and revealed, communicates in silence, and calls and gifts us with transformation. He also describes in unforgettable power and insightfulness the bride's love-filled desire, her surrender to strong love, and her immersion in God's beauty. Finally, in chapter eight, we study the image of God in the *Spiritual Canticle*; John's rich presentation of the Trinity's love for the world, the Trinity's strategy of love in dealing with humanity, and the Trinity's union in love with the soul. The conclusion draws together the overriding theme of the *Spiritual Canticle*, namely the search for union in love.

The *Spiritual Canticle* presents us with an invitation to give greater meaning to our lives, a meaning that comes from appreciation of a horizon of life beyond this one that gives meaning to this one. John is challenging, and we will need perseverance, since the early stages of the journey are not enough to satisfy desire and love. He calls us to seek the same experience he had; not more knowledge or information about God, but personal transformation and divination. This will mean leaving aside all that is not conducive to life with God and pursuing all that is of God. At a time when there are so many childish approaches to religion, John calls us to leave aside religion's trivia and to mature as total human beings and to fulfill our destiny of life in union with God. The *Spiritual Canticle* reminds us that "now that you have come to know God, or rather to be known by God" (Gal 4.9), you must open yourself to transformation. In the past we often wanted ourselves more than we wanted God, and we blocked God out of our lives. The *Spiritual Canticle* reminds us that God is the primary Lover and longs for us to give ourselves in union. It is one of the most thrilling presentations of humanity's call and destiny; the great invitation of ultimate human fulfillment.

CHAPTER ONE

JOHN OF THE CROSS: MODEL OF LOVE AND POET OF LOVE

The Life and Ministry of John of the Cross

The future John of the Cross was the third child, all sons, of Gonzalo de Yepres and Catalina Alvarez.[1] John was born in 1542 in Fontiveros, a small Castilian town of about 5,000 inhabitants, situated approximately 24 miles northwest of Avila. Gonzalo came from a wealthy family of silk merchants, and he frequently visited Fontiveros as part of his work as a regional manager for his family. There he met Catalina, and they fell in love and married. This outraged Gonzalo's family who expected that he would marry into money and not give his heart to a poor orphan girl. They disowned him and disinherited him. However, Gonzalo and

Catalina treasured the quality of their love more than wealth and built their family life on profound love that reached out beyond their immediate family to poor and needy people around them. That love should take precedence over all else became a wonderful life-lesson for the young John.

When Gonzalo died and also one of the three boys, Luis, Catalina gave her entire life in loving dedication to the growth and religious formation of her two remaining sons. She sacrificed everything, travelling to three cities in search of work, humbling herself with Gonzalo's family as she sought help from them for her children, while living in poverty and insecurity. She eventually settled in Medina del Campo around 1551, and John would spend thirteen years there in schooling, study, and training for various kinds of work. Following the example of Catalina, John seemed particularly suited for the service of the sick and needy in the hospitals of Medina del Campo. At the same time he found he had ability and love for education, culminating in his time at the Jesuit College in the city. John learned especially from Catalina the fundamental values of poverty, self-sacrifice, concern for others, a constant focus on the needy, and above all the importance of strong love. The double focus on the love of God and the love of others flourished in John from his early years and became even stronger as the years passed.

By the time he was twenty, John had had many experiences and opportunities, but more than anything he sought to direct the whole of his life to attain union with God in love. He discovered that no particular kind of work, no form of service, no institution, and no amount of study can lead one to God. John decided to enter the Carmelite monastery in Medina del Campo where he was professed as Br. John of St. Matthias. He felt called to prove his love in the rigors of the earlier, stricter observance of Carmelite life and received permission to do so. In 1564 John went to Salamanca to pursue his theological studies. Although he was an excellent student and learned much about theology, he also appreciated that intellectual knowledge does not bring one closer to God but only the personal pursuit of loving union with God. Towards the end of his third year in Salamanca John passed through a creative crisis regarding the role of contemplative prayer and contemplative life and the call he felt to seek a deeper union with God in love. He continued to live by what was known at the time as the primitive rule and gave himself to penance and prayer to prepare himself for greater union with God. He thought of joining the Carthusians to further his contemplative commitment, but in 1567 he met Mother Teresa of Avila in Medina. She urged him to help her lead the reform of the male branch of Carmel and assured him that this would help fulfill his hopes for contemplative life. John was always motivated by what he saw as the most loving thing to do, seeking God through the darker periods of life, the "nights," to union in love and renewal of life.

In the summer of 1568, after a year's preparation, John and his companion, Fr Antonio de Heredia, started the first house of the reform in Duruelo. In silence, solitude, and prayer, John and his companion began their new life around work, community, ministry, and especially prayer. Duruelo offered opportunities for penance, sacrifice, simplicity, solitude, and above all the focus on the singular pursuit of the love of God. As numbers increased in the community and Teresa and her followers opened new foundations, John's ministry of formation and outreach in service to people in the region expanded. However, in 1571, John was called to serve as chaplain to the larger monastery of nuns of the Incarnation in Avila, where Teresa had been appointed prioress. John was only in his thirties but already a well-respected theologian, reformer, novice master, confessor, exorcist, and visionary. Most of all he had a mature spiritual life enriched by deep experiences of the Lord's love.

However, along with the reform and the opportunities for deeper prayer and union in love, problems were developing especially as a result of conflicts between the various religious authorities of the day. These resulted in an attack on the monastery of the Incarnation in which John and a companion were taken prisoner. This was the beginning of a period of profound suffering for John (1577-78) who was eventually taken to Toledo, the capital of Spain at the time, and forced to face a trial on his decision to support the reform. John was condemned and spent nearly nine months in prison, most of it in a nine by five feet cell, with only a tiny window high in one wall. He suffered from hunger, frostbite in winter, searing heat in summer, deprived of the liturgy, psychological dereliction, and abandoned by his own. Three days a week he was given only bread and water. On Wednesdays he was given a public lashing by the community, he was not allowed to wash and not even given a change of clothes in the first six months. In spite of this deprivation and degradation, John never criticized his tormentors, but accepted his experiences in light of God's ongoing call to dedicate his life in love. He lived in darkness, nakedness, emptiness, and abandonment but discovered beauty and love through these experiences. While in prison he wrote some of the most love-filled poetry of all time and he emerged transformed in love.

John decided he would never be freed from his captors, and so he decided to flee from his prison. When John escaped from prison he made his way to Almodovar for a meeting of the reformed friars (1578) and from there to Beas and on to El Calvario where he led the community away from austerity to moderation and to a greater emphasis on contemplative prayer. His life was then filled with community responsibilities, extensive travels, and spiritual direction. But even this period was not one of peace and mutual support, for John experienced misunderstanding and persecution from inside the reform. John became ill and eventually went to a larger community, Ubeda, where he could receive better care, at least that was the hope. But John was made unwelcome and mistreated until the arrival of Fr. Antonio de Heredia who insisted on adequate treatment for his first companion in the reform. John's illness worsened and he died on December 14th 1591, at the age of 49. Death is the last opportunity to manifest the values of one's life, and John's death was a model of union with God in love.

John was a person of profound love and this love overflowed into his ministry. From his earliest years he had always shown compassionate concern for those in need, whether spiritual or material. His mother Catalina had taught him to always share with those in need, even giving them what he personally needed. His hospital service was a special training and opportunity for him, and he maintained love for the sick, later his sick friars, as a special focus of his service of others. He showed his loving service especially by his ministry of leading people to a deeper relationship with God. While he wrote poetry as an expression of his own inner spirit and as a support in times of hardship, his writings were always responses to other people's real needs and concerns. When you read John's works you always think he has someone in mind as he writes, and sure enough his loving concern for his directees is evidenced on every page. John's ministry is not to large groups but generally one-on-one in personal direction, and you can easily see his deep concern and love for each person with whom he deals. The prologues to his major works articulate very clearly that his motivation for writing is to help others for whom he has genuine affection and longs for their spiritual growth. He writes his letters and the *Sayings of Light and Love* to support others in their struggles, and these sayings evidence a loving concern that is very special. John's life and ministry manifest profound love at every stage. He is a model, teacher, guide, and witness of love.

Poet of Divine and Human Love

It is common to suggest that John offers two aspects of one integrated journey to God. *The Ascent of Mount Carmel* and the *Dark Night* emphasize the journey of faith, and the *Spiritual Canticle* and the *Living Flame* focus on the journey of love. These are not separate journeys but two aspects of the one journey of love-filled faith or faith-filled love and they can be summed up in the challenge of strong love. In this section, we leave aside his major works to focus on other poems and writings that focus on love. The poem of the "Dark Night," the basis for both the *Ascent* and the *Dark Night*, like the *Song of Songs*, has no immediate religious dimension; rather it is a love poem, describing the encounter between two lovers. *The Living Flame of Love* describes the final stage of union in love.

The Romances

These are an important part of John's theological vision, synthesizing his understanding of God's strategy of love in salvation history. Focusing on God's plan for the world, they complement the disciple's return journey to God which John describes in his major works. These romances are the point of departure for John's vision of life with God and act as a prologue to all his other work. Everything John presents as our return journey to God is modeled on God's journey to us as described in these romances. These nine ballads present poetical reflections on the Trinity, Incarnation, and humanity's redemption through love. One author appropriately describes them as "the Gospel of John of the Cross."[2] These beautiful poems portray the vision of the eternal life of God, the shared love in the intercommunication of the Trinity, their love-filled gift of creation, the incarnation, and Jesus' ministry of love. John presents the history of salvation as a project of love, overflowing from the Trinity's inner life of love. One commentator points out that these romances, "provide a wider narrative and doctrinal framework for San Juan's whole poetic enterprise, and link the passionate and sensuous encounter of the two lovers in the liras with the divine Trinity's embrace of all humanity through use of the same fundamental image, the marriage."[3]

The first romance portrays the inner life of the Trinity in its eternal, atemporal, mutual loving. They are bound together in eternal love, "an inexpressible knot"; the eternal begetting of the Word is an act of love by the Father, and their sharing of love is the Holy Spirit, so that there is "one beloved among all three." This part of John's vision is foundational for the disciple's return journey to God.

> 1,v.6 As the lover in the beloved
> each lived in the other,
> and the Love that unites them
> is one with them,
>
> 1,v.7 Their equal, excellent as
> the One and the Other;
> three Persons, and one Beloved
> among all three.
>
> 1,v 8 One love in them all
> makes them one Lover,
> and the Lover is the Beloved
> in whom each one lives.
>
> 1,v.11 Thus it is a boundless
> love that unites them,
> for the Three have one love
> which is their essence;
> and the more love is one
> the more it is love

The second romance deals with the internal communication among the persons of the Trinity. It is a communication in love, already heralded as the basis for the Father's love of the Son's future disciples. The Father's love for the Son is so strong that He wishes to love all that the Son loves, and this sets up the basis for all future spirituality; "My Son, I will give myself to him who loves you, and I will love him with the same love I have for you, because he has loved you whom I love so." This is part of the dynamism of love that by its very nature always wants to extend itself.

> 2,v.1 In that immense love
> proceeding from the two
> the Father spoke words
> of great affection to the Son
>
> 2,v.3-4 My Son, only your
> company contents me,
> and when something pleases me
> I love that thing in you;
> he who resembles you most
> satisfies me most
>
> 2,v.5 And he who is like you in nothing
> will find nothing in me.
> I am pleased with you alone
> O life of my life!"
>
> 2,v.7 My Son, I will give myself
> to him who loves you,
> and I will love him
> with the same love I have for you,
> because he has loved
> you whom I love so.

The third romance is a dialogue between Father and Son, the former wanting a bride for the Son, the latter wanting a bride who glorifies the Father.

> 3,v.1 My Son, I wish to give you
> a bride who will love you.
> Because of you she will deserve
> to share our company.

> 3,v.5 I will hold her in my arms
> and she will burn with your love,
> and with eternal delight
> she will exalt your goodness.

This extension of love seems so right that in the fourth romance the Father proclaims, "Let it be done." This is the first reference to spiritual marriage as a reflection of the life of love in the Trinity—the bride is all creation. Thus, creation becomes a project of love between the Father and the Son, and the love we find in the world is the epiphany of God's love.

The promise of the fourth romance continues the theme of creation. It portrays creation as a loving gift from Father to Son, a way in which the Father can love the Son even more. Creation is so overwhelmingly rich because of the Father's extraordinary love for the Son. The bride here refers to all creation, heavenly and earthly, who the Father intends as a gift of love to the Son, but whom the Son intends to return to the Father as a further sign of the Son's love. In this gamble of love by God, the Son is so desirous of showing the world how to love the Father that he decides to become part of the world himself.

> 4,v.1 Let it be done, then said the Father,
> for your love has deserved it;
> and by these words
> the world was created.

4,v.10 For he would make himself
wholly like them,
and he would come to them
and dwell with them;

4,v.15 Tenderly in his arms
and there give her his love;
and when they were thus one,
he would lift her to the Father.

For as the Father and the Son
and he who proceeds from them
live in one another,
so it would be with the bride;
for, taken wholly into God,
she will live the life of God.

The promise of the fourth romance, a promise of love, becomes the hope of the fifth and sixth, a hope portrayed in terms of longings of humanity for God. John describes the world's yearnings and expectations for the transforming love of God. After all, God's dealings with the world are undertaken to awaken our love for God. This hope culminates in Simeon's recognition of the light that descended from the heights, in the sixth romance.

The seventh and eighth romances describe the Incarnation, in which the lover becomes like the one he loves. The Father urges the Son to become like his bride, and the Son responds in love to the Father by willing the Incarnation. The Father stresses the need for likeness to create perfect love between lovers, "that the lover becomes like the one he loves," a theme John will develop in the *Spiritual Canticle*. The eighth romance concludes with the loving obedience of Mary

7,v.5 That the lover become
like the one he loves
for the greater their likeness
the greater their delight.

7,v.6 Surely your bride's delight
would greatly increase
were she to see you like her,
in her own flesh.

7,v.10 I will go seek my bride
and take her upon myself
her weariness and her labors
in which she suffers so;

7,v.11 And that she may have life
I will die for her,
and, lifting her out of that deep,
I will restore her to you.

The ninth romance brings the hope, the plan, and the promise into history through the revelation of the conception and birth through the mother, Mary. Thus, the Son comes to his bride and the world is turned upside down because of the love of the Father and the Son; "such an exchange; things usually so strange." This romance concludes in the extraordinary betrothal of the baby by his mother to humanity; "Men sang songs and angels melodies celebrating the marriage of two such as these."

9,v.2 Embracing his bride
holding her in his arms,
whom the gracious Mother
laid in a manger. . .

> 9,v.6 In God, man's weeping,
> and in man gladness,
> to the one and the other
> things usually so strange.

There is a tenth romance, a commentary on psalm 137, "By the waters of Babylon," which is not directly linked to the other nine, but it portrays the psalmists pain, hope, and longing for God's deliverance, for salvation in Jesus. John writes this in the first person, and it becomes an appropriate expression of John's own love and longings for deliverance from his prison in Toledo. "I begged love to kill me. . . I died within myself for you."

> 10,v.14 And he will gather his little ones
> and me, who wept because of you,
> at the rock who is Christ
> for whom I abandoned you.

Five popular poems/gloss

John wrote five popular poems. "I entered into unknowing" is a poem of eight stanzas that describes an ecstasy experience in contemplation. This journey of unknowing transcends all knowledge. It is a further poetical description of the purification referred to in the *Ascent* (Bk II).

"I live, but not in myself" describes how the soul suffers with longing to see God. It sounds like typical love songs of the day in which one longs to be with one's lover, transposed in this case to a soul's longing to be with God: "I cannot live without God." This present life is an imprisonment, "no life at all," in fact, "I pity myself, for I go on and on living"; "I am dying because I do not die." Partial experiences of God's presence, as in the Eucharist, help, but also remind one of the pain of absence "since I do not see you as I desire." The poem contains similar expressions of painful longing as we see in the *Spiritual Canticle* (stanzas 6-12). "Do not send me any more messengers." Even the little I see revealed leaves me dying "of, ah, I-do-not-know-what behind their stammerings." The bride describes the pain of "not living where you live." She feels wounded, her heart stolen, and left abandoned. As in the present poem, the bride in the *Spiritual Canticle* cries "reveal your presence" for "the sickness of love is not cured except by your very presence and image." But this comes only in eternity, when the soul can say "now I live because I do not die."

"I went out seeking love" substitutes the image of hunting for prey instead of longing for love. It is a secular poem to which John gives a religious interpretation (a lo divino). It describes the pursuit of love, "this adventuring in God." The motivation for this journey, this hunt, is love alone. However, John knows pains and darkness are part of this journey, "since I was seeking love the leap I made was blind and dark." John next refers to the method of the pursuit, "the higher I ascended . . . the lower and more subdued and abased I became." However, one must seek love "with unfaltering hope," "this seeking is my only hope." In a hunt, one pursues a future catch of prey. In the spiritual hunt one refocuses life to purify hope. Seeking temporal love never satisfies but leads to frustration. But "the hope of heaven attains as much as it hopes for."

"Without support yet with support" describes one's attitudes and commitment in the spiritual journey. When one journeys "without support" of any created things one will then discover that he or she is "with support" of God. This is the journey of strong love, for it implies "living without light, in darkness." This short poem to which John gives a religious interpretation (a lo divino), describes the disciple's longing for the love of God. The three stanzas successively focus on faith, hope, and charity. One's faith leads a person to abandon everything except the pursuit of God. One's hope for of heaven gives meaning to this life. One's love turns everything to goodness, a delightful flame that transforms the whole of life.

"Not for all beauty" is a secular poem that takes on extraordinary meaning for John who identifies beauty as the essence of God. Once a disciple has experienced the beauty of God nothing else will ever bring satisfaction. The main metaphor of the poem is food and eating and John compares all the delights of this world to those of "I-don't-know-what" of the next life. The former bring no satisfaction, "they tire the appetite and spoil the palate." This is because "He who is sick with love. . . finds his tastes so changed." He becomes sick of all creatures and "cannot find contentment except in the Divinity." The poem describes "a person so in love, who takes no delight in all creation," but longs and hopes for a loving union beyond this world's limitations, "for I-don't-know-what which is so gladly found."

Two special poems

"A lone young shepherd" is a beautiful secular love poem that John transposes to a religious level (a lo divino). The shepherd is Christ and the shepherd-girl is humanity. Thus, the poem is an expression of the foundational story of Christianity: the good shepherd who gives his life for those he loves. His love is so strong he willingly lives in pain, "his heart an open wound with love." What brings pain to the shepherd is that in spite of his love for humanity, men and women frequently forget him, they ignore or draw away from his love, and they do not seek the joy of his presence. Nevertheless, his love continues, "he bows to brutal handling in a foreign land," and even goes to death on the cross to show his love. The poem describes the selfless love of the shepherd and gives no sign of the shepherd-girl's love. It is a reminder of how the shepherd-girl is redeemed from a loveless life by the redemptive love of the good shepherd.

"For I know well the spring that flows and runs" is a particularly beautiful poem that describes the soul who rejoices in knowing God through faith. John wrote this poem while in prison in Toledo, probably around the octave of the feast of Corpus Christi. He had been deprived of the Eucharist for six months, living in his dark cell, with little light and overwhelmed by darkness. He can hear the rhythmic flowing of the river Tagus outside his cell. In this poem he professes his experience of God through faith in the Trinity; the Father—the eternal spring, without origin, whose bottomless love nurtures the world; the Son, "the stream that flows from this spring" and the Holy Spirit, "the stream proceeding from these two." Then John affirms that his entire faith in God is now expressed in the Eucharist, "this living bread for our life's sake," that satisfies us totally. He concludes "This living spring that I long for, I see in this bread of life." This is an expression of John's faith totally permeated by love. He weaves biblical themes of living water and bread of life throughout this beautiful doctrinal presentation. He ends each stanza with the insistent refrain "although it is night." He can satisfy his thirst for God "although living in darkness, because it is night." Night for John is guiding, transforming, tranquil, and leads to the union of the dawn.

Sayings of Light and Love

Among John's shorter prose compositions we find the *Sayings of Light and Love*, a collection of spiritual maxims that John used to give to his directees who then often copied them and passed them on to others. While written in prose there is a lyrical beauty about many of them. The structure of the sayings is very simple but not monotonous, and many are extraordinary in successfully condensing John's spiritual vision in a single statement. Some are quite poetical (number 16), some are maxims for life (60), advice in confronting dangers (66), or prayer (50). The major themes of the sayings are the necessity of spiritual direction, denial of one's appetites, the importance of being guided by reason rather than by feeling or taste, the nature of authentic love, and intimacy with God. One saying that is sometimes included with the others but not always is the "Prayer of a soul taken with love." This saying, which some writers consider autobiographical, develops in a continuing crescendo from the misery of sin, to humble abandonment, to confidence in Jesus, and finally to the enthusiastic possession of everything in the Lord.

John wrote these sayings on light and love because he felt motivated by love to do so, and he wrote them to speak to others' hearts and to stir them to greater love and service (*Sayings of Light and Love*, Prologue). John urges us to seek God with simple and pure love (2), in purity and single-mindedness (12), submissiveness (13), secrecy (20), urgency (32), and a complete focus on God's will (73) and Christ's cross (102). In order to journey in love, John says we need to be aware of our burdens and weaknesses (4), seek guidance for the journey (5), accept dryness and suffering (14), and move ahead with growing detachment (15, 43). We will need to focus every effort on God alone and take care of even small failures (23), maintain our rootedness in God (39), keep distance from this world's business (58) and other people's affairs (61), and always leave aside what is not conducive to life with God (79).

Our journey to deeper love needs to be at God's pace without us becoming attached to our own goals or ways (40-41); we will need patience and a robust spirit (42), fortitude (95), attentiveness (44), constant purification (49), self-denial (51), a re-education of the faculties (55), and awareness of the next life (83) and final judgment (77). This great journey of life is an undertaking we pursue with patience (120), a contemplative spirit (121), and constant purification of imperfections (122). As we journey we must live in the presence of God (124, 142), with genuine self-surrender (128), always walking in solitude (136), with an unselfish heart (137). Thus we will be mindful of others and never speak badly of them (148), rather, speaking of them with kindness (151), and appreciating their gifts (47).

Since God loves us so much we must be forgiving of others (47), as we make our journey in God's company (53), giving priority to the love of God above all else (54). Daily we reflect on God's love and care (86), maintain confidence (89), and live in the presence of God (90). It is important that we practice frequent self-examination (105), accept whatever trials come our way (94), concentrating always on God's love (93). With enthusiasm for God (16) we must journey peacefully in tranquility (28), gentleness and patient humility (29), centering our lives on the Word of the Son (100) and imitation of him (157), realizing all we have has come from a loving God (108).

One of the especially beautiful and love-filled sayings is the "Prayer of a soul taken with love" in which the soul prays for God's help in the pursuit of love, knowing God will always be with the person who seeks love. The soul urges readers to start immediately in the pursuit of deeper love, to do everything for God's love, and to be singularly committed to discover the God of love.

The following are a few of the *Sayings* that focus particularly on love.

16. "O sweetest love of God, so little known, whoever has found this rich mine is at rest."

60. "When evening comes, you will be examined in love. Learn to love as God desires to be loved and abandon your own ways of acting."

68. "Take God for your bridegroom and friend and walk with him continually; and you will not sin and learn to love, and the things you must do will work out prosperously for you."

78. "If you desire that devotion be born in your spirit and that the love of God and the desire for divine things increase, cleanse your soul of every desire, attachment, and ambition in such a way that you have no concern about anything."

88. "Preserve a loving attentiveness to God with no desire to feel or understand any particular thing concerning him."

97. "The soul that walks in love neither tires others nor grows tired."

115. "Love consists not in feeling great things but in having great detachment and in suffering for the Beloved."

129. "The soul that has reached the union of love does not even experience the first motions of sin."

We begin our study of the *Spiritual Canticle*, John's commentary on the exchange of love between the soul and Christ, described in stanzas that "were obviously composed with a certain burning love of God" (C. Prologue.1). We can look forward with excitement and enthusiasm, for we are being guided by one who was trained in love, lived in love, experienced deep union with God in love, and poured out his inner spirit in some of the most wonderful love poetry of all time. John has already made the journey he wants us to make, and he is a sure guide for us in our pursuit of union with God in love.

CHAPTER TWO
THE SPIRITUAL CANTICLE

Introduction and history

The *Spiritual Canticle* is an extraordinary poem and commentary, filled with the thrill, excitement, and longing of two lovers. At times it is fast-paced, moving with impatient love and longing, and at other times it is slow-paced, as the two lovers spend time enjoying each other's company. John started the poem in prison in Toledo, and there are indications that this is John's own journey of love (see C. 27.8; 28.8; 36.4). The poem begins with the lover's cry of pain at perceived abandonment. "Why have you left me? Where have you hidden, my love? Why did you leave so soon after filling me with your love?" The first five verses describe painful purification in the lover's yearnings and search. "Tell him I love so much that I am sick, I suffer, and I feel near death without him." With verse six the scene changes from purification to illumination in contemplation. "This love-sickness I feel cannot be healed except by your presence, my love." Spiritual betrothal starts with verse twelve, but the bride-to-be barely gets chance to yearn for deeper union before the bridegroom urges her to go back to further purification, telling her she is not ready for the union for which she longs. With verse twenty-two the period of spiritual marriage begins, "The bride has entered the sweet garden of her desire." And from verse thirty-six we read of the final period of intense longing for full union in eternity. "Let us rejoice, my love, and go forward to behold ourselves in your beauty."

The bridegroom only speaks in seven of the forty verses, telling the bride-to-be of her need to return to more purification (13), promising his further protection of the bride as a continuation of his redemptive love on the cross (23), and celebrating her persevering love and solitude (34-35). The bridegroom is certainly more absent than present, seems to ignore the bride's pleading, and teases her with brief periods of presence. The bride speaks in thirty-two of the forty verses, expressing pain at her lover's absence (1), her determination to search relentlessly until she finds him (2-5), her intense longing for direct contact with her lover (6-11), and her joy in finding him (12). She celebrates his many qualities (14-15), the gifts she receives from him, including his protection and his help in controlling her sensory disturbances (16-19). Above all she rejoices in the union of spiritual marriage, the revelations of the mysteries of God and the inner life of God's beauty (22-24). However, she also appreciates the virtues of her own life—all gifts from her Lover, and the communication of his intimacy, tenderness, and love. In fact, she celebrates their mutuality in love, their total mutual surrender, her transformation by her Beloved, and their union and joy (25-33). Finally, cherishing the union they now have, she looks ahead to deeper union in eternity (36-40).

The *Spiritual Canticle* is John of the Cross' longest poem (200 lines—the *Dark Night* has 40, and the *Living Flame*

24) and also his favorite. He wrote the poem in prison when surrounded by rejection and ugliness, and he celebrated in the poem the wonders of love and beauty. It begins and ends his work as a writer (1578-1586), in fact, he refers to the upcoming publication of the works of Mother Teresa of Avila which was in 1586 (see C. 13.7). He wrote the first 31 verses in prison in Toledo—he was thirty-five years old—and the last nine verses on three other occasions.[4] The commentary, his first doctrinal synthesis in prose—*Spiritual Canticle* is first in 1579, the *Ascent* and the *Dark Night* early in 1580— he wrote bit by bit, ending in Granada in 1584.[5] He then touched up the text for another two years, giving us the definitive text in Los Martires, Granada, in 1586.[6] In the *Spiritual Canticle* John looks back over the spiritual life, perhaps his own, and interprets it from the perspective of love. However, the ongoing editing was hardly thorough and detailed since John was not preparing anything for publication. The title is not John's but that of his first disciples and biographers. Fr. Jerónimo de San José used this title in his 1630 edition of John's works.[7] However, the title seems to reflect John's own approach, even though he called his work "songs" (canciónes) and the commentary a declaration or explanation (Déclaración de las canciónes).

As a result of John's constant editing and reinterpretations, we now have two editions of the *Spiritual Canticle*, both poem and commentary. Both are now considered authentic, the second does not supplant the first but makes different choices.[8] The first edition or redaction (A) follows the logic of love; the structure of the second (B) is more pedagogical. The first has 39 stanzas, the commentary is shorter, the quotations are in Latin, the last five stanzas seem to speak of an earthly perfection attained through mystical marriage, and the poem and commentary are more spontaneous and lyrical. The second edition (B) has 40 stanzas; John added stanza 11 and changed the order of 18 intermediate stanzas (16-33 in B).

Redaction A	Redaction B
1-10	1-10
	11
11-14	12-15
15-24	24-33
25-26	16-17
27-28	22-23
29-30	20-21
31-32	18-19
33-39	34-40

The commentary of B is longer and more logical; John adds an introduction at the beginning of most sections, and annotations before each stanza. The last five stanzas are more clearly related to eternal life of which mystical marriage is a foretaste. The second version is doctrinally more valuable and manifests greater clarity and order. It refers to the *Living Flame* (C. 31.7) and thus was written after it (1585-86). All codices of the *Spiritual Canticle* indicate that it was written at the request of Ana de Jesús, prioress of the Discalced Carmelite nuns of St. Joseph's in Granada. The commentary is not divided into chapters or books, as are the *Ascent* and *Dark Night*, but simply follows the stanzas of the poem.

John wrote the poem as an expression of his own spiritual journey during those difficult but love-filled nine months in the Toledan prison. He seems to have composed the verses gradually, reciting them to support and give expression to his spiritual integration, until a new jailor gave him writing materials, and he then transferred his poetry in written form. This was sometime in December 1577 to August 1578. Mother Magdalena del Espíritu Santo testified that when John left prison she saw a notebook of his containing stanzas for the *Spiritual Canticle*.[9]

The commentary was a response to requests for an explanation of the poem. We are told that when John was confessor to the nuns in Beas de Segura, he lent them a notebook of poems and Magdalena del Espíritu Santo made copies of them. The nuns were deeply affected by them and asked for an explanation. As a result John started short paragraphs of explanation while still working on the *Ascent*. While these notes were preliminary to the complete text, John's secretary, Fr. Juan Evangelista, testified that without doubt John wrote the commentary to the *Spiritual Canticle* in Granada, beginning and ending it during Fr. Juan Evangelista's time with him. Even the completed work states that "It was written at the request of Mother Ana de Jesús." So, John wrote the commentary because he was asked to do so. It does not seem that he was too attracted to this task. "Who can describe in writing the understanding he gives to loving souls in whom he dwells? And who can express with words the experience he imparts to them? Who, finally, can explain the desires he gives them? Certainly, no one can" (C. Prologue.1). In the prologue to the *Living Flame*, John tells us that he is reluctant to explain the poem in detailed commentary, and that seems to be his sentiment here too.[10]

The commentary has a logical development following the traditional stages of the spiritual life, but the poem has a back and forth movement, more integrative than progressive. The commentary is didactic and developmental, the poem sees the whole all at once and the poet sees the end from the beginning. The former has an ordered doctrinal development; the latter presents a lyrical disorder, more visible in A than in B. Mother Teresa of Avila never read the commentary, since it was written after her death. However, she did read the poem, often, and recommended it to her sisters.

Outline of the Spiritual Canticle

There are four stages in the composition of the *Spiritual Canticle*. First, there was John's own personal spiritual experience of loving encounter with God. Second, there was the re-living of this experience in the composition and re-reciting of the stanzas of the poem.[11] Third, there was the ordering of the stanzas into a coherent spiritual journey. Fourth, there was the subsequent redaction of the commentary following the ordering and re-ordering of the poem.

John explains the four major divisions in stanza 22 of the B redaction (C. 22.3): 1. An anxious search for the loved one (stanzas 1-12); 2. The joy and preoccupation of the encounter with the loved one—spiritual espousal (stanzas 13-21); 3. The total union, insofar as is possible in this life, and resulting fruits—spiritual marriage (stanzas 22-35); 4. Desire and glory (stanzas 36-40). In this book we will use redaction B. The following may serve as a working outline.[12]

Spiritual Canticle

Title and dedication.

Prologue: John describes the purpose and limitations of his work.

The poem: A dialogue between the bride and Bridegroom.

Theme: General statement about the work.

Part I. An anxious search for one's Lover (stanzas 1-12)

Part I describes the early stages of searching for union with God. This begins with purification and initial contact with God through intermediaries, but one must arrive at the point of a deliberate decision to pursue union. One starts by seeing God's presence all around, appreciating the divine presence in creation, and finding one is called to love God above all else. This partial experience of God is inadequate and painful, and one becomes restless for greater union, especially when one sees the beauty of God and senses one is called to transformation and union. There are two sections: 1. The journey begins in pain and purification (1-5). 2. The phase of contemplative illumination (6-12).

Part II. Encounter with one's Lover in spiritual betrothal (stanzas 13-21).

Part II describes the period of spiritual betrothal which is an in-breaking of God's transforming love and includes special communications of God's loving presence. The individual feels protected from previous disturbances, but also feels the pain of the absence of the Lover. One now sees one's own gifts, longs for transformation of spiritual faculties, and yearns for the deeper union of the next stage—spiritual marriage.

Part III. The experience of union in spiritual marriage and its resulting fruits (stanzas 22-35).

Part III describes spiritual marriage which is a profound transformation of the individual. It is a revelation of special secrets and brings gifts of union. It includes an appreciation of God's gifts to others. It is an experience of peaceful security, mutual surrender, and equality in love. It focuses on love alone in mutual self-gift. God makes all this possible, for God is love. God purifies former failures, and this leads to mutual gratitude and rejoicing.

Part IV. The desire for fullness of union in eternity (stanzas 36-40).

Part IV describes the two lovers' longing for total union in glory. This includes immersion in the mysteries of God, delight and gratitude, participation in the life of God, and complete harmony in union with God.

The outline can be helpful in guiding us through the reading of the poem and text. However, these are not rigid divisions. We will see how the various sections of the *Song of Songs* contain similar themes in each of its sections. While the *Spiritual Canticle* develops in clearly defined stages, from purification, to illumination, to transformation, to union, and to further longing, it is also clear that recurring themes are present throughout. So, each of the four parts of the *Spiritual Canticle* speaks of longing, purification, progressive revelation of God, the pain of absence and inadequate union, the conviction that only God's love suffices for us, the two lovers' deepening mutual, self-gift, and the joy of loving union with God.

Language of love in the Spiritual Canticle

John of the Cross is unquestionably the mystical doctor of divine and human love, and nowhere do we see this better than in the *Spiritual Canticle* which treats of the entire spiritual life exclusively from an affective perspective. It shows us the growth of love from early anxieties and yearnings to God's illuminative guidance and teachings on love, and on to the in-breaking of God's love into the searching soul. It then proclaims the intensity of union between the lovers in mutual peace, surrender, and self-gift, and speaks of the Lover's gift of equality in love.

In the Toledo prison, John experienced mystical union in love and felt the urge to proclaim it in the verses of the *Spiritual Canticle*, and later to share it. Mystics long to share their experiences as a sign of their love for God whose love they experienced and in appreciation of the divine gifts they have received. They have a profound desire to express their experience and in doing so they enrich it and re-live it. John's first biographer, Jerónimo de San José, mentioned an episode in the prison, that one night John, who was in low spirits, heard a young man singing a love song in the street outside. "I am dying of love, dearest, what shall I do? Die." After Toledo and Almodóvar, John stopped at Beas de Segura on his way to El Calvario. Mother Ana de Jesús said he was like a dead man, and she asked one of the nuns to sing. The nun sang: "He who knows nothing of pain in this valley of sorrows, nothing knows of good things nor has tasted of love, since pains are the garment of lovers." John asked her to stop and clung to the bars of the grille for over an hour overcome with emotion. He then told the nuns how God had taught him the value of suffering.

The *Spiritual Canticle* describes the trajectory of love from one who has experienced it, and John is not just a love-poet, but a lover. "[T]here is an abandonment to all the sensations of love, which seems to me to exceed, and on their own ground, in directness and intensity of spiritual and passionate longing, most of which has been written by love-poets of all ages. These lines, so full of rich and strange beauty, ache with desire and all the subtlety of love. . . this monk can give lessons to lovers."[13] At first, John was reluctant to write about this experience and echoed feelings he expressed in the *Living Flame*. "I have felt somewhat reluctant . . . to explain these four stanzas. . . since they deal with matters so interior and spiritual, for which words are usually lacking. . . I find it difficult to say something of their content...." (F. Prologue.1; see also A. Prologue.1 and C. Prologue.2). Language is so important to us for communication, for development of relationships, and for our own growth as individual human beings. It is particularly important in matters of religion where we transmit vital experiences through the language of faith. Sometimes expressions of faith end up as just words, and we then lose the reality behind the words. John was concerned that the powerful experiences of love not be lost in mere words. Thus, John comments on the efforts of some who went before him. "The saintly doctors, no matter how much they have said or will say, can never furnish an exhaustive explanation of these figures and comparisons, since the abundant meanings of the Holy Spirit cannot be caught in words. Thus, the explanation of these expressions usually contains less than what they embody in themselves" (C. Prologue.1).

People who have had a profound spiritual experience generally find it difficult to explain it to others in precise language. Often this is because they do not fully understand it themselves, or their explanation always seems to fall far short of the experience. Sometimes they use symbolic or suggestive language to explain their experiences. John himself pointed this out, "everything I say is as far from reality as is a painting from the living object represented" (F. Prologue.1). Because of this difficulty, mystics often use figurative expressions rather than rational explanations. "These persons let something of their experience overflow in figures, comparisons, and similitudes, and from the abundance of their spirit pour out secrets and mysteries rather than rational explanations" (C. Prologue.1).

Thus, John can also advise us: "As a result, though we give some explanation of these stanzas, there is no reason to be bound to this explanation. For mystical wisdom, which comes through love. . . need not be understood distinctly in order to cause love and affection in the soul, for it is given according to the mode of faith through which we love God without understanding him" (C. Prologue.2). He comments further: "It is better to explain the utterances of love in their broadest sense so that each one may derive profit from them according to the mode and capacity of one's own spirit, rather than narrow them down to a meaning unadaptable to every palate. As a result, though we give some explanation of these stanzas, there is no reason to be bound to their explanation" (C. Prologue.2). So, conceptual and speculative language may help to clarify and articulate our faith, but its vital core—our loving relationship with God—is more truly shared "in mystical theology which is known through love and by which these truths are not only known but at the same time enjoyed" (C. Prologue.3).

John's major works begin with figurative titles—ascent, dark night, canticle of love, living flame—titles that already evoke responses in the hearts of believers. John then presents his poems as glimpses into his profound experiences: "unable to express the fullness of his meaning in ordinary words, [he] utters mysteries in strange figures and likenesses" (C. Prologue.1).[14] When disciples ask John to explain these poems he starts with a prologue in which he states that it is not possible to explain adequately the experiences to which the poems refer. Appreciating mystical language in its many expressions requires ascetical commitment. "Spiritual joy directed to God at the sight of all divine or profane things follows from the eye already purged of enjoyment in seeing things" (A.3. 26.5). So, as we read John, we must remember that "these words are spirit and life. These words are perceived by souls who have ears to hear them, those souls, as I say that are cleansed and enamored" (F. 1.5).

The *Spiritual Canticle*, both poem and commentary, is filled with vivid language, rich imagery, and an extraordinary beauty of expression. It presents a passionate intensity of language, is filled with the tensions of love, and sometimes immerses us in the irrationality of the expressions of love. At times it seems autobiographical, and the dialogue between the bride and bridegroom, or the soul and God, sounds like a dialogue between John and God. It seems we are witnessing John's cry of anguish at the abandonment he felt in prison, or his joy in the union of love. In the prologue to the *Spiritual Canticle* John tells us that the poem is "composed with a certain burning love of God," is "composed in a love flowing from abundant mystical understanding," and that only the "fruitful spirit of love" will release its full meaning, for it is written for "loving souls in whom he dwells." These "utterances of love," are a form of mystical wisdom that "comes through love," and are presented "in order to cause love." This commentary is written for those whom the Lord has led "into the depths of his divine love," those who are "wounded now with love of God," and are filled with "longings of love."

In the first part of the poem and commentary the bride tells us that she is wounded with love (20 x), that she feels touches of love (4 x), and an internal fire of love (3 x). She says she feels longings of love, is sick with love (5 x), her heart stolen through love (5 x), and she even feels she is dying with love (7 x). She speaks of her lover as "he whom my soul loves" (5 x), through love she leaves all creatures for his love (3 x), seeks him in faith and love (2 x), and senses she is transformed in his love (2 x). She describes her love as authentic, impatient, ardent, vehement, and says that her lover slays her with the force of his love. John focuses his teachings with some remarkable sayings on love, expressed with power, elegance, beauty, and profound challenge. "Nothing is obtained from God except by love" (C. 1.13). "[L]ove seems to be unbearably rigorous with the soul" (C. 1.18). Through her desires, affections, and moanings, the soul manifests "the secret of the lover's heart" (C. 2.1). He tells us that "the lover does not possess her heart but has given it to the beloved" (C. 9.2). In fact, "The wages of love are nothing else. . . than more love, until perfect" (C. 9.7). Now the soul realizes that "Her work is to love" (C. 9. 7), and this can bring sickness for "love in incurable except by things in accord with love" (C. 11.11). "The reason for this is that love of God is the soul's health," and "the soul does not have full health until love is complete." So, the first part comes to a conclusion with the soul's awareness that "In the measure that love increases she will be healthier and when love is perfect she will have full health" (C. 11. 11).

In part two the bride continues to speak about the wounds of love (4 x) and touches of love (2 x) but now emphasizes the transformation of love (6 x), union of love (6 x), and the idea that love produces likeness (2 x). She refers to the Holy Spirit who is love (4 x), the bridegroom's tokens of love, and the need for strong love. She describes her yearnings and ardors of love (2 x) and says that her love is now burning (3 x), vehement, but also peaceful and sweet (2 x). She also speaks of the delight and gentleness of love (2 x) and the refreshment of love. This section on spiritual betrothal is special to John who tells us "the Beloved lives in the lover and the lover in the Beloved" (C. 12.7). He says the bride would endure any pain so that "she could plunge into the unfathomable spring of love" (C. 12.9). He tells us that the Bridegroom visits his bride "with strong love amid the intense longing desires" (C. 13.2), and the bride responds, "I am refreshed and renewed in the love" (C. 13.2). This will always be so, "for in the lover, love is a flame that burns with a desire to burn more" (C. 13.12). In this section the bride prepares her heart so that her Lover "may enter through the complete and true 'yes' of love" (C. 20-21.2).

In the section on spiritual marriage, the unitive part of the journey of love, John's language of love is especially significant, at once passionate and powerful, and yet sweet and delicate. This is a time of praise, rejoicing, and intimacy. The bride learns more about her Lover (4 x), enjoys his visits of love (2 x), and drinks deeply of his love. However, this is also a time of mutual surrender, transformation (4 x), and consummation. The bride becomes absorbed in love, burns up with love, and becomes inebriated with love. Above all she now experiences union and communion in love (9 x) and enters into perfect love (10 x). The love is at times a spark, a touch, lofty and ardent, but also sweet, solitary, and like balsam. However, it is also fortified and strong love. She speaks of loyal and mutual love, gentle and complete love, tender and true love, supreme and generous love. She feels bathed in love, enjoys the sleep of love, appreciates the treasure of love, and is immersed in desire, love, praise, and reverence. At this time, the Beloved "inflames her in the fire of love" (C. 25.5), the Father favors her with "the tenderness and truth of love" (C. 27. 1). In response the bride "knows how to do nothing else than love and walk always with its Bridegroom in the delights of love" (C. 27.8). She appreciates that "there is no greater or more necessary work than love" (C. 29.1). John knows that "Anyone truly in love will let all other things go in order to come closer to the loved one" (C. 29.10). The result is extraordinary, "God was intimately taken with love for her" (C. 31.3), "he should be satisfied and captivated by her love" (C. 31.10); in fact, "The power and tenacity of love is great, for love captures and binds God himself" (C. 32.1).

The final part is both a continuing celebration of mutual love and an anticipation of a life of union in glory. It is a time to receive, to rejoice, and to let love overflow into the practices of life. John speaks about the fruition and delight of love, the glowing tenderness of love, deeper communication of love, and the consummation of love. The bride and Bridegroom celebrate their mutuality in love, he shows her how to love, she realizes her love becomes God's loving in her, and she experiences immersion in the life and love of the Trinity. Love is now profoundly intimate, strong, transformed, consummate, and perfect. John reminds us that "lovers cannot be satisfied without feeling that they love as much as they are loved" (C. 38.3). Then he adds a thought that sums up much of the *Spiritual Canticle*, "the ultimate reason for everything is love" (C. 38. 5).

Reading the Spiritual Canticle

1. Identify with John of the Cross

John was a very knowledgeable theologian, an outstanding spiritual director, and a good biblical exegete with the methods of his day (see A.2. 16-22).[15] He could develop a sustained argument full of understanding from Scripture, theology, spirituality, and spiritual direction. He was equally remarkable in his analytical skills, discrimination, and discernment. He read extensively and in the *Spiritual Canticle* was influenced by two main sources—the *Song of Songs* and Garcilasco.[16] Often he presents concepts from both, linked, woven, or fused together—perhaps not always deliberately but certainly rooted in the back of his mind.[17] And yet John is quite unique and one cannot confuse his style with any other writer; his style and methods indicate a strong, independent personality.

The three phases of his work—poetry, commentary, revisions—indicate his work develops gradually from verses, notes, paragraphs, and chapters that are then included in his final work without much change. His poetry can be viewed as autobiographical,[18] and yet he even struggles to explain them and refers to his own experiences as "stammering," "I-don't-know-what." It is filled with an abundance of images that develop to describe search, betrothal, marriage, and deeper longings for union. John's use of images in the *Spiritual Canticle* is not as clear as in the *Dark Night* or the *Living Flame*; he uses the same image for different objects and sometimes applies to the bride what he later applies to the Bridegroom. It is interesting how John comments line by line on his poems, like a scholar doing biblical exegesis, thereby giving the poems a special status. Allison Peers describes John's work as "the most grandiose and the most melodious spiritual canticle to which any one man has ever given utterance."[19] Brenan speaks about "the intoxicating effect these poems produce."[20] Thompson refers to John as "a man who seems to be writing twentieth-century poetry 400 years before its time."[21] Certainly, in reading this book we must, first of all, appreciate the genius of the author.

2. *The environment in which John wrote*[22]

John wrote the poem of the *Spiritual Canticle* in prison in Toledo and the commentary in Andalusia. In Granada, he lived close to the opulence of the Alhambra, surrounded by a new class with their vices and pretentions; a city with slaves, camps, and brothels, and with the memories of the persecutions of the Moriscos. He lived during the reign of Philip II and his ambitious expansionism, religious wars, and his people's growing poverty due to heavy taxes. He also lived during the Council of Trent and the subsequent reforms of the Church. In its pursuit of reform and orthodoxy both Teresa and John would face the challenges of the Inquisition, the former regarding the prayer of quiet, and John regarding the similarities between the *Spiritual Canticle* and the *Song of Songs* which was frowned upon by the Inquisition. So the *Spiritual Canticle* was excluded from the first edition of John's works in 1618. In fact, it is worth mentioning that in the *Spiritual Canticle* John seems to avoid anything that could give rise to suspicion and misinterpretation.[23]

But this was also a time of reform for various religious orders including the Carmelites for whom reform meant going back to a more primitive observance and laying aside all the mitigations of the rule as was understood at the time which had arisen for various reasons. John's own experiences, his work in formation and spiritual direction, and his writings, all evolve in the atmosphere of Carmelite reform. In this context, so much of John's insight in his works comes from his extensive experience in ministry to the needy, in spiritual direction, in his interactions with laity wherever he worked, and in the progressive maturing of his own spiritual life. Of course the time in which John lived gave more emphasis to storytellers, poets, troubadours than we do today. The sharing of religious poetry was common, and it is important to acknowledge that poets, including John, touch a level of consciousness that others do not.

3. See the whole picture

Part of John's genius is his ability to see the whole picture. The night is dark, guiding, more lovely than the dawn. Suffering is part of total transformation. The active nights of the *Ascent* need the passive nights of the *Dark Night*. Even on a practical level, when John went to found a new house he had an integrated vision of all the needs. When others took sides he could see the complementariness of Teresa, Gracián, himself, and Doria—with of course some notable exceptions. Above all, as we see in the *Spiritual Canticle*, his teaching is very demanding but this is all part of the demands of love—to love nothing but what God loves.

When John of the Cross writes any of his works his system of spiritual development is already complete, at least in his own mind. He may write other works later, but these are explanations for others not for him. Everyone lives based on convictions that form a systematic way of approaching life—whether they realize it or not, whether they can articulate it or not. John has a very clear understanding of the systematic development of the spiritual life and how each part relates to others in a progressive development. Part of John's genius is his ability to see the whole picture. So, when John writes to his directees he locates his advice within the context of the systematic development of the spiritual life (see L. 3 and 13, S. 19, 23, 25). In the *Spiritual Canticle* we meet the bride who already refers to the one she seeks as "him I love most." And she describes intense, loving union long before the spiritual betrothal. When she reaches an experience of union, she is told to go back to further purification. So, John sees the whole picture of the spiritual life and how each part fits in with the whole picture.

4. Do not obscure John

There will be times when we might let ourselves be put off by the language and ideas that John uses, but we must separate his culturally restricted presentations from the perennial values of the realities of the spiritual life. The simplest form of obscuring the message is to read in English without appreciating the different language, culture, and religious outlook that can still remain. Part of this problem is interpreting John within our own restricted contexts, whereas John employs a new world of thought, imagination, images, sensations, feelings, memories, and will that are not ours.[24]

One of the ways we obscure John's thought and challenges is by presenting him as a theologian of the Church of his time, as if he agreed with the official party line. This domesticating of John eviscerates his message. The Church fought John and tried to condemn him, right up to his canonization. Even nowadays there are some who like to keep John within manageable spiritual realms, rather than appreciating that he calls us to face the dark nights of the Church and society.

John is a wonderful poet, one of the greatest, but his interest is not beautiful poetry but an awesome religious experience. We cannot get caught up in the language, art, lyricism, and beauty, but confront the challenges of the spiritual life that he brings to us.

We can sometimes obscure the full power of John's challenge when we too easily persuade ourselves that some texts apply to us. John is not a general practitioner in the spiritual life but a specialist, and his teachings need careful application. We are wise to get a knowledgeable spiritual director.

5. *Attitudes of the reader*

In reading the *Spiritual Canticle* it is important not to worry about secondary, unimportant issues, such as style, unusual vocabulary, terminology, culturally restricted concepts and practices, historical problems of the time. After reading the beautiful poems one can get lost in didactic presentations of the commentary with its tangle of themes, digressions, and repetitions. We need to keep our focus on the main lines in the spiritual life which are clear to John from the start, even though they may not be immediately clear to us.[25]

In reading John we enter his interests with humility and hope, and with a willingness to accept the purification necessary to appreciate what is happening in the journey. We should be aware of our own need, emptiness, and longing to know the answers to our life questions. We should not only read, but listen attentively, aware that it is a privilege to hear what he has to say, and we need to be worthy.

We come to John being at peace with strange concepts, with simplicity of spirit, seeking to enter the circle of love that he creates. We should approach his teachings in mutual friendship with him, willing to be empty and receptive, establishing a communion between him and ourselves, appreciating that he is a great teacher of love.

In the *Spiritual Canticle* as in the *Song of Songs* readers are invited to participate. The lovers in the poems are not embarrassed to share their love and to let others know about it. So, reading this special work can re-conjure love as we read it and call us to think of our own love relationships with others and with God. As we read the *Spiritual Canticle* each of us can join in the love relationship as the primary participant, identifying with the emotions of the writer, so that we too are satisfying our longings in pursuing deeper love.

Each of us comes to the *Spiritual Canticle* with our own history, and John leaves the reader to read and be influenced by God telling us that the poetry is open to multiple interpretations (C. Prologue.2).[26] So, each of us can be open to writing or at least imagining our own personal commentary and applications.

CHAPTER THREE
THE SPIRITUAL CANTICLE AND THE SONG OF SONGS

Scripture's love poem

The *Song of Songs*, attributed to Solomon, appears in the third part of the Hebrew bible, the "writings" or "hagiographa," while in the Greek and Latin translations it appears with the wisdom literature, since like them it is dedicated to Solomon. "Song of songs" means "the best of all songs," and it certainly is a beautiful poem or collection of poems. From time to time, some commentators have suggested the poem was written early, especially by those who consider it a poem written for one of Solomon's marriages, or because of its references to Tirza as capital of the northern kingdom. However, in general, given its use of Aramaic and Greek words, most commentators consider this book of the Bible as post-exilic, while accepting the possibility that individual parts or sections could be earlier. Both Jews—

from the time of Rabbi Akiba at Jamnia in CE. 90—and Christians have always accepted this as a canonical book of the Bible. However, concerns about the appropriate use of this book have been common throughout history, as one would expect, given the fact that it never mentions God once, does not deal with explicit religious issues, and is filled with erotic imagery.

Those who have been or are disturbed by the erotic imagery and believe that such imagery could not be part of a sacred book of the Bible have tried to salvage the book's place in Scripture by interpreting it as an allegory or parable that dramatically describes God's love for humanity; the latter is the bride and the former the groom, while the "daughters of Jerusalem" become the world that looks on in awe at the relationship of love between God and humanity. Christians have also viewed the poem as describing the relationship between Christ and the Church, and in liturgy have suggested that the bride is Mary, either individually in her love for God's will or as a symbol of the Church in relation to Christ. The trouble with these approaches is that there is not much structure, plot, or storyline in the book, since it often gives the impression of being a jumbled collection of short poems. Moreover, the *Song of Songs* gives no indication of being anything other than a collection of love poems. Many interpretations given of individual passages have been forced in their authors' efforts to give a religious coat of paint to a poem of human love and sexuality.

Some commentators identify five or six separate love poems while others prefer to speak of a collection of up to twenty five to thirty sayings concerning the relationship of two lovers. The collection is unified by the theme of love, by the dramatic pursuit of deeper intimacy, by continuous dialogue between the bride and groom, by a refrain (2:7; 3:5; 8:4), and by recurring themes, ideas, and key words. At first reading the *Song of Songs* describes the relationship of two young lovers and their desire for increased intimacy—from flirtation, lovesickness, and fear of loss, to sensuous and sexual longings. These themes are certainly not inappropriate in Scripture or in the Church, both of which have always seen conjugal relationships as blessed by God and integral to human development. However, the poem is unquestionably very powerful and calls readers to think beyond the goodness of human love. Of course, even married couples often find that their own love points to something beyond the immediacy of their relationship. When dealing with texts, in this case biblical, passages and entire books take on a life of their own in the hearts of believers. Readers establish the agenda for interpreting the passages. Because the poem's original and immediate meaning refers to erotic love does not mean that readers need to remain at that level. Rather, the book has clearly taken on a life of its own in the history of spirituality. This is not simply allegory, but the critical assessment of readers' responses. It is not surprising that this love song challenges readers to think of God's love for humanity.

There are various ways of viewing the structure of this book, but several writers consider the book to be divided into five or six significant sections:

1:1-4 Introduction: the bride's longing for her lover
1:5-2:7 First poem: a dialogue of mutual praise
2:8-3:5 Second poem: the bride longs for her beloved, he invites her to accompany him to the fields, she returns home and her longing to see him again increases (This is the woman's first long speech).
3:6-5:1 Third poem: the two lovers are portrayed as king and queen, the groom is enthralled by the beauty of the bride (A continuation of the woman's first speech together with the man's first speech).
5:2-6:3 Fourth poem: the lover knocks on the door of the bride's room but by the time she opens the door he has gone.

She then searches for him throughout the city, praising him to anyone she encounters (The woman's second speech).

6:4-8:4   Fifth poem: the two lovers express their praises for each other and their unswerving love (The man's second speech and the woman's reply).

8:5-7   Conclusion: the two lovers are inseparably united

8:8-14   Appendix: A dialogue about love: the bride's brothers try to prevent the union, but the bride reaffirms her choice for her beloved

Human love as an image of divine love

These poems are not progressive from the first to the last, but rather they deal with similar themes of longing, pursuit, discovery, mutual praise, self-forgetfulness, desire to be together, anxiety, deeper longing, satisfaction, and so on, and these themes appear in each of the poems. All poems also have images from nature—mountains, valleys, rivers, fountains, and flowers, as well as physical, sensual, and erotic images. In the Song of Songs the two lovers are archetypal images of lovers, and the poem does not focus on who they are but on the quality of their love. It describes the intense desire for mutual love, and the poem has no closure, no end to their longing. We learn about the challenge of love in the lovers' own words. Their dialogue gives a sense of immediacy, as if we are observers, attentive to what they can teach us about love. Both are continually desiring each other and being desired by each other. While there may be problems around them, their only focus is their mutual love and all else is secondary.

In spite of their images and content, writers throughout the history of spirituality have found this book of Scripture to be one of the most powerful to express the believer's longing for God. Of course, readers must have the right attitudes in their reading. Spiritually sensitive people will discover awesome challenges in the poems, while others will not get beyond the erotic imagery. For a couple in love, this song suggests love, conjugal sexual love for some, but definitely love. It is interesting how mystics and spiritually dedicated people can be comfortable with its imagery when others less spiritually focused cannot. For most of us the meaning of the poems is not exhausted in the erotic, while for some the meaning is not erotic at all but a description of total intimacy and so an excellent image of union with God. Since the two lovers represent all lovers, the poem can readily be used as a presentation of the love between God and a believer.

Often in life ordinary events of each day challenge us to think about values beyond the ordinary in a realm of life beyond this one. At times, we have experiences of the excessive richness of life that open us to a horizon of life beyond this one. Examples could be childbirth, creativity, forgiveness, and the beauty of this world. Some experiences could stunt our lives, or make us attentive to the apparently diminishing transcendent experiences; among these would be vulnerability, death, failure, loneliness, and alienation. Then again, there are moments in our service of others that call us to think of lasting values—experiences like war, working for justice, liberating the oppressed, and working with the poor. In each case an ordinary everyday event helps us focus on values in a world beyond this one.

However, the one experience more than any other that naturally challenges us to think about the realm of life that is beyond this one and gives meaning to this one is any experience of genuine love. To love someone or to be loved by someone makes us realize that we are loveable, that we want to be loved, and that others too are loveable and want to be loved. We see humanity as loveable, and we appreciate a level of the mystery of God's love for us all. Through the events of every day, the God of love calls us all to appreciate that everyone has meaning only within the mystery of love. At times we may not be able to express this conviction even though we readily appreciate it when someone else expresses it for us. Thus, we see the perennial attachment of humanity to love songs or to the poetry of love. The "music of the night," in the Phantom of the Opera surely calls us to values beyond the experiences of the phantom and Maria: "silently the senses abandon their defenses. . . Grasp it, sense it, tremulous and tender. . . Close your eyes, let your spirit start to soar. . . Let your mind start a journey through a strange new world." John of the Cross was also impressed by some secular, love poems, and transferred them to a spiritual level (a lo divino). The best example would be the poem that describes the love of a lone young shepherd.

We appreciate love more than anything else for it is a manifestation of what is deepest within us and what we know we need to be. Love is so special to us, and when someone expresses it for us we are thrilled. We appreciate it, long for it, and think we are our best when we show it. When we reflect on the beauty of human love, it makes us think about the unconditional and unmerited love of God for humanity. When spiritual writers over history read the *Song of Songs* they found it to be a wonderful expression of a believer's search for meaning, longing for fulfillment, thrill of meaningful presence, mutuality, intimacy, and union, and the blessings that result from this pursuit.

The earliest commentary on the *Song of Songs* was written by Hyppolytus (170-235), then one also by Origen (184-253). In the fourth century Gregory of Nyssa wrote his commentary. Since John wrote the *Spiritual Canticle* in Granada, of particular interest is the commentary by Gregory, Bishop of Elvira (Granada), towards the end of the fourth century. In the middle ages this was the most commented book in the monasteries, and there were a series of commentaries from writers like William of St. Thierry, Bernard of Clairvaux, and others. Around the time of John of the Cross (1561), his teacher, Luis de León, prepared a new translation and wrote a commentary for his sister.

In our generation we too often restrict eros to sexuality, whereas it is a drive for union and completion that extends to the pursuit of knowledge, wisdom, life, and spirituality. Pope John Paul II in commenting on the theology of the body presented a major section on the *Song of Songs*, and Pope Benedict XVI in his encyclical, "God is Love," did the same—each accepting both a literal and an allegorical interpretation of this biblical book. The *Song of Songs* starts with the former but naturally and almost immediately gives rise to the latter. Its four tempos translate readily to the spiritual life: search, encounter, union and satisfaction, and longing. We will find these four tempos in John's *Spiritual Canticle*, corresponding to the four sections. The *Song of Songs* is an extraordinary powerful challenge to think about God's love for us and our longing to be in union with God.

John's use of the Song of Songs in the Spiritual Canticle

John of the Cross quotes from the Old Testament 684 times, of which 117 are from the *Song of Songs*, and 67 of these are in the *Spiritual Canticle*. When John wrote the *Spiritual Canticle* there was no Spanish translation of the *Song of Songs* available, and he would have used the Latin. However, John quotes with such ease that several commentators suggest he may well have known it by heart. One author, commenting on John's use of images and quotes, says; "Those which he had taken from the "Song of Songs" had long been meditated by him and interpreted to fit his mystical experience, so that he would have had many of their meanings in his head before he began to write."[27] John recognized the Bible as authoritative and inspired in every part and as a source of illumination for us in our lives. He used Scripture more as revealed symbols of our own life and calling, rather than as we do today in our contemporary literary critical approach. He used stories from Scripture as archetypes of our own stories, as symbolic expressions of common human experiences. Since the two lovers in the *Song of Songs* represent all lovers, John could readily use the poem as a presentation of God and the believer, and given its use in history this would be the only interpretation that writers like John would think of. Besides the special focus on the lovers' relationship, John's *Spiritual Canticle* also shares the *Song of Songs'* emphasis on pastoral themes, the beauty of nature, the lovers' mutual appreciation, and lots of similar vocabulary and themes.

The *Song of Songs* may well be a collection of independent sayings on love, but it is now unified in its focus on the same two lovers. The editor has now permeated each section with the same constantly mentioned themes: the lovers continually desire each other and are desired by each other, they long for union, they become forgetful of themselves and lose themselves in each other, they are anxious in their longing and when satisfied immediately long for deeper union. John's *Spiritual Canticle* is much more carefully organized and structured than the *Song of Songs*. It has four sections corresponding to stages in the spiritual life, and each of these has a rhythm and tempo of its own. The four tempos translate readily to the spiritual life: search, encounter, union and satisfaction, and longing. We see these in each of the sections of the *Song of Songs*, and they appear like waves, constantly coming towards us in poem after poem. We will find these four tempos in John's *Spiritual Canticle*, corresponding to the four sections. So, John chooses quotes from the *Song of Songs* according to his four sections.

Part I of the *Spiritual Canticle* deals with the anxious search by the bride for her Beloved. There are twelve quotes from the *Song of Songs* in this first part, and all of them refer to the theme of constant search for one's Lover. John chooses his quotes from four of the five poems in the *Song of Songs* together with the conclusion, identifying with the theme of constant search in each of the sub-poems. Part II of the *Spiritual Canticle* (stanzas 13-21) deals with the bride's encounter with her Beloved, an encounter that results in joy and satisfaction together with some preoccupation that she might lose his presence. There are twelve quotes in this part, six refer to encounter, five to joy, and two to preoccupation, and again they are taken from the five sub-poems together with two from the appendix. Part III of the *Spiritual Canticle* presents the total union of spiritual marriage and the resulting fruits (stanzas 22-35). There are thirty-four quotes in this section, eighteen on union and sixteen on the fruits of union, and John chooses the quotes from every section of the *Song of Songs* except the appendix. Part IV (stanzas 36-40) deals with the two lovers' longing for total union in the glory of the next life. John uses eight quotes in this part all on the theme of longing for deeper union. He quotes from four of the poems and the conclusion.

	C. Part I Search and longing	C. Part II Encounter and preoccupation	C. Part III Transformation and union	C. Part IV Further longing
Intro: 1:1-4			1, 2, 3	
1st poem: 1:5-2:7	1, 2	1	1, 2, 3, 4, 5, 6, 7, 8	
2nd poem: 2:8-3:5	1, 2, 3, 4	1, 2, 3	1, 2, 3	1, 2, 3
3rd poem: 3:6-5:1	1,	1, 2	1, 2, 3, 4, 5, 6, 7, 8	1
4th poem: 5:2-6:3	1, 2, 3	1, 2	1, 2, 3	1
5th poem: 6:4-8:4		1, 2	1, 2, 3, 4, 5, 6, 7	1, 2
Conclusion: 8:5-7	1, 2		1, 2	1
Appendix: 8:8-14		1, 2		

The *Song of Songs* begins with a kiss and ends with withdrawal and absence, as the lover flees like a stag. The *Spiritual Canticle* starts with absence and the lover fleeing like a stag, and it ends in union. The four themes in each of the sub-poems are brought together in John's four parts of the *Spiritual Canticle* and present a powerful confirmation of these stages in the spiritual life. 1. We must begin the spiritual journey with an intense longing for God and a willingness to do whatever it takes to pursue union. 2. When we encounter God, we can immediately celebrate the preliminary union of spiritual betrothal, a transforming experience that still leaves us a little preoccupied. 3. We rejoice and celebrate the total transformation in the union of spiritual marriage, sense the security, mutual surrender, and equality in love. 4. We also experience that desire and longing never seems to end in this life, and we are always yearning for more. The two lovers in the *Song of Songs* have an initial experience of this. John builds on this and enriches it in his presentation of the four stages in the call to undertake, endure, and celebrate this profound journey of love.

Appendix: Specific quotes used by John and his interpretation of them

Part I. Stanzas 1-12: The Anxious search for one's Lover.

There are twelve quotes in this first part and all of them refer to the theme of constant search for one's Lover.

Tell me, you whom my soul loves, where you pasture your flock, where you make it lie down at noon (SS 1:7). Twice

The soul seeks the vision of God, and God's manifest presence in the divine Word. [C. 1.5, 6]

My beloved is like a gazelle or a young stag (SS 2:9).

God comes and then leaves and the soul thinks of a swift stag who appears and disappears. [C. 1.15]

"I will rise now and go about the city, in the streets and in the squares; I will seek him whom my soul loves." I sought him, but found him not (3:2); I sought him, but did not find him; . . . they wounded me (SS 5:6-7).

The soul rises and goes out from a lowly state of loving to one more sublime, which is experienced as a wounding. [C. 1.21]

Upon my bed at night I sought him whom my soul loves; I sought him, but found him not; I called him, but he gave no answer. "I will rise now and go about the city, in the streets and in the squares; I will seek him whom my soul loves" (SS 3:1-2).

I sought him. . . [and] I found him (SS 3:4).

The soul will not find God unless she goes out in search of God. [C. 3.2] This search is filled with trials but eventually the soul will find God. [C. 3.2]

I adjure you, O daughters of Jerusalem, if you find my beloved, tell him this: I am faint with love (SS 5:8).

There are three ways of getting to know God each with its own kind of suffering. The first is simply a wound that heals quickly; it is the knowledge of God that comes from creatures. [C. 7.2]

You have ravished my heart, my sister, my bride, you have ravished my heart with a glance of your eyes, with one jewel of your necklace (SS 4:9).

The second way of knowing God produces its own pain that is like a sore wound that cuts more deeply; it is produced by knowledge of the incarnation and the mysteries of the faith. These produce a more intense love. [C. 7.3]

I sought him, but did not find him; I called him, but he gave no answer. Making their rounds in the city the sentinels found me . . . they wounded me, they took away my mantle, those sentinels of the walls (SS 5:6-7).

The soul encounters three sets of problems in his or her search. The soul experiences the "sickness of love," as he or she is always seeking and not finding the loved one; second the soul loses taste for everything else, and third she finds everything else to be burdensome. "Those who make their rounds in the city" are the distracting affairs of the world; "the sentinels" who prevent the soul from entering into contemplation are the evils and preoccupations of the world that destroy one's peace. [C. 10.3]

We will make you ornaments of gold, studded with silver (SS 1:11) reference not a direct quote.

Faith gives us an incomplete knowledge of God; it is not perfect (all gold) but partial (gold covered with silver). [C. 12.4]

Set me as a seal upon your heart, as a seal upon your arm (SS 8:6).

Transformation in this life is partial but still pleasing to God who wants the soul to place such longing as a seal on the soul. [C. 12.8]

For love is strong as death, passion fierce as the grave (SS 8:6).

This describes the intensity of painful longing the soul experiences in his or her search for God. [C. 12.9]

Part II. Stanzas 13-21: Encounter with the Loved one, resulting joy and satisfaction, and yet some preoccupation.

There are twelve quotes in this part, five refer to encounter, five to joy, and two to preoccupation.

Let me hear your voice; for your voice is sweet (SS 2:14).

The soul rejoices to hear the spiritual voice of God; a communication that produces great delight. [C. 14-15.11]

My fancy set me in a chariot beside my prince (SS 6:12).

The text used by John has a different translation: "My soul was disturbed because of the chariots of Aminadab", and John suggests Aminadab is the devil and the chariots refer to his attacks and assaults. [C. 16.7]

Catch us the foxes, the little foxes, that ruin the vineyards— for our vineyards are in blossom (SS 2:15).

Having withstood the attacks of evil the soul experiences the flowering of virtues that he or she recognizes as shared with the Beloved. [C. 16.7]

While the king was on his couch, my nard gave forth its fragrance (SS 1:12).

When the Beloved is at rest in the soul of the bride, the latter gives the groom satisfaction of presence. [C. 17.8]

Awake, O north wind, and come, O south wind! Blow upon my garden that its fragrance may be wafted abroad (SS 4:16).

The soul prays that the Holy Spirit, the divine breeze, blow through her virtuous life and bring the smell of this flowering to the Beloved. [C. 17.9]

My beloved has gone down to his garden, to the beds of spices, to pasture his flock in the gardens, and to gather lilies. . . I am my beloved's and my beloved is mine; he pastures his flock among the lilies (SS 6:2-3 –two references).

The bridegroom unites himself with the soul who is in flower with virtues. [C. 17.10]

We have a little sister, and she has no breasts. What shall we do for our sister, on the day when she is spoken for? If she is a wall, we will build upon her a battlement of silver; but if she is a door, we will enclose her with boards of cedar (SS 8:8-9).

The soul that has inadequate development of the virtues of purity, fortitude, and love will need the defenses of heroic virtues, a strong soul, and lofty love to prepare for spiritual marriage. [C. 20-21.2]

I was a wall, and my breasts were like towers (SS 8:10).

The bride replies to the previous reservations by stating her soul is strong and her love lofty. [C. 20-21.3]

"Who is this that looks forth like the dawn, fair as the moon, bright as the sun, terrible as an army with banners?" (SS 6:10).

The bridegroom illuminates in the bride the gifts he has previously bestowed and those who see it marvel. [C. 20-21.14]

A garden locked is my sister (SS 4:12).

The bridegroom sets up a fence, protecting the bride from troubles and disturbances. [C. 20-21.18]

I adjure you, O daughters of Jerusalem, by the gazelles or the wild does: do not stir up or awaken love until it is ready (SS 3:5).

Let the bride freely enjoy the sleep of love. [C. 20-21.19]

Part III. (Stanzas 22-35): Total union and resulting fruits.

There are thirty-four quotes in this section, eighteen on union, and sixteen on the fruits of union.

Come out. Look, O daughters of Zion, at King Solomon, at the crown with which his mother crowned him on the day of his wedding, on the day of the gladness of his heart (SS 3:11).

The groom rejoices that the bride has been freed from sensuality and evil, and he urges others to rejoice with him. [C. 22.1]

I come to my garden, my sister, my bride; I gather my myrrh with my spice (SS 5:1).

The bridegroom rejoices that the bride has reached transformation. [C. 22.5]

O that you were like a brother to me, who nursed at my mother's breast! If I met you outside, I would kiss you, and no one would despise me (SS 8:1).

The bride tells the bridegroom how much she longs for spiritual marriage. [C. 22.7]

For now the winter is past, the rain is over and gone. The flowers appear on the earth (SS 2:11-12).

The bride rejoices that appetites and passions are subdued and she reaches the fulfillment of spiritual marriage. [C. 22.7]

Under the apple tree I awakened you. There your mother was in labor with you; there she who bore you was in labor (SS 8:5).

As the bride was born under the crime of the tree, so now the bridegroom brings her life under the tree of the cross. [C. 23.5]

I am a rose of Sharon, a lily of the valleys (SS 2:1).

The bride says their bed is in flower, flourishing, and the bed on which she rests is the Son of God. [C. 24.1]

Our couch is green (SS 1:16).

The bride likens the union with God in love to a bed in full blossom. [C. 24.3]

O that you were like a brother to me, who nursed at my mother's breast! If I met you outside, I would kiss you, and no one would despise me (SS 8:1).

The bride enjoys security in participation of God freed from all disturbances, passions, and temporal cares. The kiss symbolizes union. [C. 24.5]

King Solomon made himself a litter from the wood of Lebanon. He made its posts of silver, its back of gold, its seat of purple; its interior was inlaid with love (SS 3:9-10, indirect quote).

All virtues are bound together by love (purple), for without such love the soul could not enjoy this bed and its flowers. [C. 24.7]

Around it are sixty mighty men of the mighty men of Israel, all equipped with swords and expert in war, each with his sword at his thigh because of alarms by night (SS 3:7-8).

The bride is crowned with the virtues she has practiced; they symbolize her reward and give her protection. [C. 24.9]

Your neck is like the tower of David, built in courses; on it hang a thousand bucklers, all of them shields of warriors (SS 4:4).

In addition to the virtues the bride practiced, God bestows a thousand more graces and gifts. [C. 24.9]

Your anointing oils are fragrant, your name is perfume poured out; therefore the maidens love you. Draw me after you, let us make haste (SS 1:3-4).

Each one makes haste according to the spirit God gives. God leaves a trace of divine love in the soul and

it acts like perfume that attracts one to follow. [C. 25.4]

My beloved thrust his hand into the opening, and my inmost being yearned for him (SS 5:4).

In the experience of union God touches the soul with divine love which comforts and cures the soul. [C. 25.6]

O that his left hand were under my head (SS 2:6).

The bride describes the happiness she feels in this state of union. [C. 26.1]

My soul failed me when he spoke (SS 5:6).

The soul expresses delight at the communications from God. [C. 26.5]

I would lead you . . . I would give you spiced wine to drink, the juice of my pomegranates (SS 8:2).

The bride receives wisdom and knowledge, and her love is transformed by the love of the bridegroom. [C. 26.6]

He brought me to the banqueting house, and his intention toward me was love (SS 2:4).

The bride shares in the very love of the bridegroom which he infuses in her. [C. 26.7]

Before I was aware, my fancy set me in a chariot beside my prince (SS 6:12).

Absorbed in the love of the bridegroom the bride is unaware of all else. [C. 26.14]

I am my beloved's, and his desire is for me. Come, my beloved, let us go forth into the fields, and lodge in the villages; let us go out early to the vineyards, and see whether the vines have budded, whether the grape blossoms have opened and the pomegranates are in bloom. There I will give you my love (SS 7:10-12).

A description of the bride's surrender to the bridegroom. [C. 27.2]

Over our doors are all choice fruits, new as well as old, which I have laid up for you (SS 7:13).

The bride insists that all that is rough and toilsome I desire for your sake, and all that is sweet and pleasant I desire for your sake. [C. 28.10]

I adjure you, O daughters of Jerusalem, by the gazelles or the wild does: do not stir up or awaken love until it is ready! (SS 3:5 indirect reference).

The soul is now immersed in love alone and the Lord urges all creatures never to disturb this sleep of love. [C. 29.1 also 29.3]

I am my beloved's and my beloved is mine (SS 6:3).

This refers to the celebration of espousal. [C. 30.1]

Draw me after you, let us make haste (SS 1:4).

The soul's movement towards good comes only from God but both need to also work together. [C. 30.6]

Come out. Look, O daughters of Zion, at King Solomon, at the crown with which his mother crowned him on the day of his wedding, on the day of the gladness of his heart (SS 3:11).

The crowns and garlands are the saints in the Church, the Bride of Christ; There are three kinds—virgins, doctors, and martyrs. [C. 30.7]

How graceful are your feet in sandals, O queenly maiden! (SS 7:1).

The bride appears marvelous to the spiritual eye because of her virtues. [C. 30.10]

You are . . . terrible as an army with banners (SS 6:4).

The bridegroom acknowledges that the bride is not only beautiful because of her many virtues but also possesses great strength. [C. 30.11]

Sustain me with raisins, refresh me with apples; for I am faint with love (SS 2:5).

The bride asks for the strength that comes from virtues and gifts. [C. 30.11]

I am a rose of Sharon, a lily of the valleys (SS 2:1, indirect reference).

The flowers represent the bridegroom. [C. 31.1]

You have ravished my heart, my sister, my bride, you have ravished my heart with a glance of your eyes, with one jewel of your necklace (SS 4:9).

The bridegroom says he is overcome with the bride's faith and fidelity (eyes) and love (jewel). [C. 31.10]

The king has brought me into his chambers. . . . I am black and beautiful, O daughters of Jerusalem (SS 1:4-5).

God sees how beautiful the bride is and then endows her with more blessings. [C. 33.7]

Ah, you are beautiful, my love; ah, you are beautiful; your eyes are doves. Ah, you are beautiful, my beloved, truly lovely (SS 1:14-15).

These are expressions of the mutual appreciation of the bride and the bridegroom. [C. 34.1]

My beloved speaks and says to me: "Arise, my love, . . . O my dove" (SS 2:10, 14, indirect reference).

John uses this reference to indicate the purity of the beloved imparted by grace. [C. 34.3]

How beautiful you are, my love, how very beautiful! Your eyes are doves behind your veil. Your hair is like a flock of goats, moving down the slopes of Gilead (SS 4:1).

John uses this reference to the dove's eyes to mean loving contemplation [C. 34.3]

With great delight I sat in his shadow, and his fruit was sweet to my taste (SS 2:3).

The bride, after all her searching and fatigues, now finds refreshment and rest. [C. 34.6]

Part IV (Stanzas 36-40): Longing for total union in glory of next life.

Nine quotes in this part all on the longing for deeper union.

I will hasten to the mountain of myrrh and the hill of frankincense (SS 4:6).

The bride longs to see herself in the beauty of God and thus be transformed into the wisdom of God. [C. 36.8]

Arise, my love, my fair one, and come away. O my dove, in the clefts of the rock, in the covert of the cliff (SS 2:13-14).

Like Moses who could only see God from a cavern in the rock, so too the soul who longs to be transformed and absorbed by love must in this life be protected by the caverns of Christ's care. [C. 37.5]

His body is ivory work, encrusted with sapphires (SS 5:14).

These are the mysteries and judgments of divine wisdom. [C. 37.7]

I would lead . . . I would give you spiced wine to drink, the juice of my pomegranates (SS 8:2).

The Holy Spirit teaches the bride about love by means of knowledge of God's attributes. [C. 37.8]

Go forth, O daughters of Zion, and behold King Solomon, with the crown with which his mother crowned him on the day of his wedding, on the day of the gladness of his heart (SS 3:11, indirect reference).

What you gave me. . . you will give me then on the day of my espousal and nuptials and on my day of gladness of heart. [C. 38.8]

Arise, my love, my fair one, and come away; for now the winter is past, the rain is over and gone. The flowers appear on the earth; the time of singing has come, and the voice of the turtledove is heard in our land (SS 2:10-12).

The bridegroom calls to the bride to make the journey to eternal life. [C. 39.8]

Arise, my love, my fair one, and come away. O my dove, in the clefts of the rock, in the covert of the cliff, let me see your face, let me hear your voice (2:13-14) . . . for your voice is sweet (SS 2:14).

The bridegroom tells the bride that evil is at an end and they can together give praise to God. [C. 39.9]

Who is that coming up from the wilderness, leaning upon her beloved? (SS 8:5, indirect reference).

The bride has come from the desert of death and is now liberated and filled with blessings. [C. 40.1]

Indirect quote concerning the armies of evil (SS 6:11)

The soul is no longer threatened by evil. (C. 40.3).

CHAPTER FOUR
THE STORY OF THE
SPIRITUAL CANTICLE —
(A summary)[1]

PART I

This commentary deals with the mutual love between the soul and Christ and develops the relationship to prayer. It is written at the request of Mother Ana de Jesús, prioress of St. Joseph's, Granada, 1584.

---

[1] See *Collected Works of St. John of the Cross*, translated by Kieran Kavanaugh, O.C.D., and Ottilio Rodriguez, O.C.D., (Washington, DC: ICS Publications, 1991), "The Spiritual Canticle," pp. 469-630. This is an effort to summarize the book of the *Spiritual Canticle*; it is about one fifth of the original length. It leaves out asides and duplicate explanations, while faithfully presenting the words and ideas that John writes. There are still some problems with language and concepts that are unusual to contemporary readers. However, in a shorter version it still gives us chance to immerse ourselves in John's context, ideas, and spiritual challenges.

Prologue

1. These stanzas were composed as an expression of love, and they deal with love, but we cannot fully express in words the depth of an experience of love—we just cannot fully understand it or communicate it to others. All we can hope for is that figures, comparisons, and suggestions can give indications of this extraordinary experience. Moreover readers will need to approach this with similar simplicity of spirit and with some of the love of which these stanzas speak. No matter how learned the saints who tried to share their experiences, their expressions were a shadow of the real experience. 2. These stanzas were composed out of mystical love, and the commentary can merely shed a little light on the experience. Mind you, suggestive language—rather than detailed explanations—is helpful in so far as each reader understands and benefits in his or her own way. This means the explanation is not restrictive but adaptable to each individual, thus producing love in each reader as appropriate. 3. The commentary will be brief with appropriate digressions especially concerning prayer. The text focuses less on beginners, since there are other works for them, and more on the extraordinary effects of prayer which seems more suitable to Prioress Ana de Jesús and her sisters. Here and there will be references to scholastic theology, but readers who are not lacking in mystical appreciation should still gain from the text. 4. John says he submits his work to the Church's authority and intends to document his ideas in Scripture. At the same time he is conscious of his own and others mystical experiences and will take them into account. John then gives the full poem.

Theme: 1. & 2. The stanzas describe the spiritual journey from the first steps to the culminating experience of spiritual marriage—purgative to illuminative to unitive stages.

Stanza 1.

Introduction: 1. The soul begins the spiritual journey with an increased awareness of evil, of the shortness of life, of judgment, of her indebtedness to God, and of the innumerable blessings of God. Feeling that her forgetfulness of God causes God to appear angry and hidden, the soul in sorrow renounces everything except to search for God and proclaims the first stanza:

Where have you hidden,
Beloved, and left me moaning?
you fled like the stag
after wounding me;
I went out calling you, but you were gone.

Commentary: 2. The soul longs for union, laments God's absence, feels wounded by unfulfilled love, and suffers in her own unworthiness, crying out: Where have you hidden? 3. She asks God to reveal the divine self that is hidden from weak humanity. But, no matter how special God's self-revelation might be, it is small in relation to who God really is. In fact, God always remains more hidden than revealed. Because we think we experience God's presence does not mean we really do, nor when we think God is absent does it verify that God really is. 4. We should never presume that a special spiritual communication truly represents God or assures us of union. Then again, when others remain empty and dry or cannot sense God's presence, they should not presume that God is absent. The soul in this verse understands these issues and is in pursuit of the presence and vision of God which only comes in fullness in the next stage of life. 5. The soul asks where God is hidden and finds that the fullness of revelation is in the Son, the exclusive place of encounter. 6. Where is God hidden? The Trinity is hidden in the innermost being of the soul and those who long to find God must leave aside all false loves and enter into the inner depths of their own beings. 7. So, the soul should not search outside of self, for deep within one's self is the hiding place of God. We can rejoice that God is so near, in fact, we are never without God. 8. God is never absent from anyone. We can rejoice that God is ever present even when we fail. So, do not become distracted or weary, seeking God here or there, when God is always within, even though still hidden. 9. Although within us, we often do not find God because God is concealed within our hearts, as in a hiding place. If we want to find God, we too must leave aside everything and conceal ourselves in the hiding place of our inner spirit. Encountering God in secret our experience will transcend language and feeling. 10. Knowing the Beloved is hidden within our hearts, we should strive to be hidden with God—that is when we experience God's love and uncover the secret mystery of faith. This encounter can never be perfect in this life, but it will lead to union with the Son and transformation in his love—a union so strong the soul will no longer need to ask: "Where have you hidden?" 11. To find God within, you must do the following: seek God in faith and love without seeking satisfaction or understanding. These attitudes will lead along an unknown path to where God lies hidden. There the soul will discover the meaning of faith and find loving union. This will always be partial—God will always be somewhat hidden in this life. 12. In this search the soul must leave aside the activities of the faculties. Rejoice in what you do not understand rather than in the little you do understand. Love what you cannot understand or experience, rather than what you do. God is inaccessible to our discovery, understanding, and experience. We are often closer when we do not understand, taste, or experience God than when we think we do. 13. In this stanza, the soul calls God "Beloved" to move God to answer the longing of the soul. It is fine to call God "Beloved" when the soul is totally with God and has no attachments outside of God. Centering all on God, the soul must persevere in prayer, set his or her heart totally on God, and remember that nothing is obtained from God except by love. 14. One can recognize a person who truly longs for and loves God if they are content with nothing except God. Perfection consists in poverty of spirit—not in possessions. Only in this poverty of spirit can one possess God in an intimate and special way. The soul still says "and left me moaning" for no matter the peace and satisfaction that comes in finding God within, the soul hopes for what she lacks and feels the pain of loss when God withdraws, leaving the soul alone and dry. 15. The soul insists "You fled like a stag," remembering how the stag is so swift—here a moment and then gone. Thus, God gladdens the soul briefly and is then gone, leaving the soul in sorrow. God does this to humble and teach the soul. 16. As one's desire for God increases, the soul feels God's absences more intensely. 17. God's many visits raise up the soul in love. God also wounds the soul with special touches of love that intensify the soul's affection and purify and renew the soul's entire way of life. 18. These special touches of love change the focus of one's appetites and affections to focus on God alone. This produces an intense and painful yearning to see God which becomes a more painful suffering when the soul realizes God has withdrawn swiftly as the stag, leaving the soul wounded and dissatisfied. 19. So, the soul rises up in love only to find God has withdrawn, and thus, feels an inability to possess God. These divine visits do not refresh and satisfy but wound and afflict in order to purify knowledge and intensify desire. Nevertheless, painful as these touches of love are, they are also delightful and desirable, drawing the soul out of self and allowing entrance into God. 20. No one can heal these wounds except God who caused them, so the soul goes out calling to God. This departure results from one's love of God and includes a rejection of everything that is not God, and a self-forgetfulness. Thus, leaving aside everything including self, the soul focuses on God alone. 21. "But you were gone." As the soul leaves aside everything to go to God, God withdraws and the soul is left without any support. In this way the soul leaves aside her immature ways of loving and is drawn to the sublime love of God. However, this movement is painful, for as the soul experiences the touch of love, God withdraws, and the soul suffers from God's absence. In loving surrender and painful loneliness the soul feels she has gained nothing from her loss and has not gained possession of the Beloved. 22. The pain arising from God's absence is intense. This experience purifies the soul and prepares it better for future union. Having tasted something of God's love, the soul suffers profoundly when it is lacking.

Stanza 2.

Shepherds, you who go
up through the sheepfolds to the hill,
if by chance you see
him I love most,
tell him I am sick, I suffer, and I die.

Commentary: 1. At first, a lover makes use of intermediaries in relating to God, especially when there are no possibilities of direct contact. Here the soul suggests that her desires, affections, and longings act as messengers of her commitment. 2. Appreciating these messengers of the lover's longings—yearnings that nourish the soul and manifest the soul's pure love—God communicates the divine self because of the quality of this love. 3. These messengers of the lover's longings rise up to God and return from God to further feed the soul with communication and inspiration and at the same time protect the soul from evil. 4. The soul hopes God will hear these signs of love and that God answers the soul's longings for communication. God only answers when the time is right. Even if God does not answer the lover's prayers immediately, the soul should not be discouraged, for when the opportune time comes God will hear the petitions. 5. The soul affirms he or she loves God more than all else, that nothing will hinder the search, and that this leads to a readiness to suffer to prove loving service. 6. The suffering the love accepts—caused by God's absence—affects the three faculties of intellect, will, and memory. The intellect fails to see God, the will to possess God, and the memory focuses on past, present, and future limited images of God. 7. The soul speaks of her poverty regarding the wisdom of God, of her bitterness regarding the will's inability to possess God, and of her sense of death without God. These three needs are connected to the theological virtues of faith, hope, and charity that reside in the intellect, memory, and will. 8. So, the soul manifests her needs to the Beloved, leaving the Beloved free to respond as he sees best. After all, the Lord knows what is best for us and has more compassion towards our needs. In this approach the soul is saved from self-love, and can simply state her needs.

Stanza 3.

Seeking my Love
I will head for the mountains and for watersides,
I will not gather flowers,
nor fear wild beasts;
I will go beyond strong men and frontiers.

Commentary: 1. The soul realizes that interventions of intermediaries are insufficient, and feels moved by intense love to try any means to bring herself closer to God, especially the practice of virtues and the spiritual exercises of both active and contemplative life. These efforts must include withdrawal from self-satisfaction and from the three enemies—world, devil, flesh. 2. The soul realizes that spiritual efforts are insufficient and must do absolutely everything that is possible in searching for the Beloved. Words are not enough, and spiritual satisfaction a hindrance. Rather, the soul needs to lay aside satisfaction, comforts, and useless desires. No one will find God unless he or she goes out in search no matter the trials. 3. Those who seek God for their own satisfaction will not find God. Those who lay aside self-satisfaction and give themselves to the practice of virtue will find Divine wisdom. 4. Climbing high mountains is an image of the heights and laborious efforts needed to practice the virtues that lead to contemplative life. The search will include the active life of self-sacrifice and penance to complement the contemplative life—both being necessary. 5. The soul leaves aside all that is not God—all forms of self-gratifications and delights whether temporal, sensory, or spiritual. Attachment to any of these hinders the single-mindedness necessary for direct contact with God and blocks the exclusive focus on the search for God. Any attachment whether temporal or spiritual becomes an obstacle to the way of the cross that alone leads to union with God. 6. The three enemies of the soul—world, devil, flesh—cause hardships along the way to God. 7. The world becomes an obstacle on this journey by filling the soul with fear that she will lose favor, friends, reputation, by leading to anxiety that such losses, together with a lack of consolation and delight, are permanent and by concern that others will ridicule her efforts. These trials hinder progress and sometimes block every initial effort. 8. Other temptations and trials arise that are more interior and spiritual—sent by God to test those who God wants to raise up to higher levels. But the dedicated soul determines to go beyond these trials. 9. The second enemy of the soul's search is the devil who tries to entrap in temptations often linked to the world and flesh—but more intense than these alone. The soul realizes he or she cannot overcome these temptations without prayer, self-sacrifice, and humility. 10. The third enemy of progress is the natural rebellion of the flesh against the spirit which the soul must overcome, otherwise this rebellion presents a serious obstacle in the journey. The soul needs courageous perseverance in withstanding the world's values, strength in overcoming temptations, and single-minded commitment never to stop the search for God.

Stanza 4.

O woods and thickets,
planted by the hand of my Beloved!
O green meadow,
coated, bright, with flowers,
tell me, has he passed by you?

Commentary: 1. Preparations for the search of the Beloved include leaving aside the delights and satisfactions of this world, overcoming temptations, and thus fostering self-knowledge. Then the soul appreciates God in the wonders of the created world. 2. All aspects of creation reveal the wonders of God's love, and the soul sees God reflected in them. 3 Aware that God alone as Creator brought forth such awesome diversity leads the soul to deeper love of God. 4. The soul meditates on the rich diversity of God's wonderful creation both on earth 5. and in the heavens, 6. where angels and saints add to the beauty, 7. for God has placed excellent qualities in all aspects of creation.

Stanza 5.

Pouring out a thousand graces,
he passed these groves in haste;
and having looked at them,
with his image alone,
clothed them in beauty.

Commentary: 1. The created world bears witness to God's grandeur, for God has placed something of the divine self in all of creation. 2. For God has endowed the whole world with innumerable graces. 3. Thus, the soul can see traces of God's presence in all the world and while these blessings are less than those revealed in the mysteries of the Incarnation, they nevertheless reveal God's grandeur. 4. For God communicates these graces in the Son, especially because the Son elevates creation by taking on human nature and thus clothing it in beauty.

Stanza 6.

Introduction: 1. Contemplating the world, the soul sees how God has clothed all in beauty so as to reflect the beauty of the Son and thus the soul is inspired to love God the source of all this goodness, beauty, and love.

> Ah, who has the power to heal me?
> now wholly surrender yourself!
> Do not send me
> any more messengers,
> they cannot tell me what I must hear.

Commentary: 2. The soul's love of God increases the more she sees the many traces of God's love revealed in creation. At the same time this becomes insufficient and the soul becomes anxious to encounter the Beloved and not just traces of his presence in creation. The soul's grief at the Beloved's absence can only be cured by union in love, 3. for the soul now knows that nothing in this world can satisfy the deep longings she feels. 4. Authentic love can only be satisfied with the possession of God. All partial revelations increase the longing without satisfying the intense desire for God. 5. All knowledge of God in this life is only partial and can never fully satisfy. 6. In fact, partial revelations increase sorrow at God's absence and seem to be delaying the desired outcome. So, the soul acknowledges that up to this time she was content with partially seeing God but no longer; now the soul wants total authentic union and no more messengers. 7. Nothing can satisfy except the satisfaction of complete union.

Stanza 7.

All who are free,
tell me a thousand graceful things of you;
all wound me more
and leave me dying
of, ah, I-don't-know-what behind their stammering.

Commentary: 1. In the previous stanza, the soul explained the pain he or she feels when given knowledge of God through irrational creatures. In this stanza she speaks of knowledge she gains from rational creatures—angels and humans. These latter reveal more about God than the former—admirable and yet still incomplete. 2. Because of this intensity of revelation, the soul suffers from love in three ways—three wounds of love. The first is mild and heals quickly. It is the pain from the love of God revealed through creation. 3. The second is more painful and lasts longer. It results from knowledge of the Incarnation and the mysteries of the faith. This is a greater sign of God's love than that discovered in creation. 4. The third experience of the pain of love seems like death to the soul, caused by a momentary experience of profound knowledge of God. This is a form of impatient love, when the soul having had this experience longs intensely for it again. 5. So, irrational creatures cause one kind of wound of love, while rational ones two other wounds from God's love in the mysteries of faith and from the moment's unveiling of the knowledge of the divinity. 6. Moreover, the rational creatures are free to seek God by contemplating and enjoying God in heaven or by loving and desiring God on earth. Through these rational creatures' teachings the soul gains profound knowledge of God, 7. for they reveal God's grace and mercy. 8. Through their inspiration and teaching they inspire the soul to love God more. 9. Certainly they teach, and yet there is so much that is unknown and still to be revealed—an understanding of God that cannot be expressed in words. Now and again God favors souls with a glimpse of divine grandeur that at once reveals and at the same time shows how much is still hidden.

Stanza 8.

Introduction: 1. When the soul receives spiritual knowledge and experience of creatures, it leads to a partial understanding of the greatness of God.

> How do you endure
> O life, not living where you live,
> and being brought near death
> by the arrows you receive
> from that which you conceive of your Beloved?

Commentary: 2. The soul longs to be united to God in love and feels restricted by bodily life that prevents total union. Life in the body deprives one of true spiritual union in love, a life that is greater than bodily life. Revelations through creatures of God's greatness are wounds of love—intense, love-filled communications that are so overwhelming that the soul longs to pass from this life to the next to enjoy this love more fully. 3. The soul lives in God's love rather than in her body and this love gives life to the body. Living in God's love, the soul is totally centered on God. The soul knows God sustains her natural life and love of God gives spiritual life. It seems to the soul that natural life is a hindrance to the spiritual life of love—the former seems like death in comparison to the latter. 4. The soul feels she must endure life in the body, overwhelmed by the touch of God's love that is so strong it seems likely to bring an end to this bodily life. God's love penetrates to the depth of her being, bringing profound knowledge of God; 5. knowledge of God's greatness, beauty, wisdom, and life.

Stanza 9.

Introduction: 1. As a wounded stag rushes around trying to find healing from its pain, so too the soul who suffers the arrows of God's love never stops seeking remedies for the pain. All efforts fail and even bring greater pain, and so the soul throws herself on her Beloved, realizing he alone can bring healing.

> Why since you wounded
> this heart, don't you heal it?
> And why, since you stole it from me,
> do you leave it so,
> and fail to carry off what you have stolen?

Commentary: 2. The soul, wounded and alone, turns to the Beloved, the only source of healing, and asks why he wounded with love and then left her in pain rather than healing her with the vision of his presence. It seems the Beloved stole the soul's heart but then leaves her helpless instead of transforming her in total loving union. 3. The wounds of love are wonderful for the soul, but she suffers from the fact the love is incomplete and cannot fully satisfy. The longing for complete union is painful and the soul will never be satisfied except in total love. 4. The soul complains that the Beloved stole her heart but then did not take full possession of her. 5. Lovers focus more on the Beloved than on self. Thus, the soul knows she loves God totally when she is always concerned with pleasing God and not self. 6. There are two signs that a soul is totally given to God: if she constantly longs for God, and if she finds no satisfaction except in God. The heart longs to possess the object of its love, and in so far as it does, it suffers from this emptiness and longing. 7. The soul prays for complete union and satisfaction. Love longs for more love until the longing for fulfillment and perfection brings complete love.

Stanza 10.

Introduction: 1. As a sick person longs for health, so the soul longs for healing of her love sickness. Her heart is always fixed on the Beloved. She loses taste for everything else, and anything else is a burden except the pursuit of love. 2. Since she has tasted God's gift of love, nothing else now satisfies her. Rather, she seeks to taste and enjoy this gift of love with no further interest in self. She seeks to find her Beloved in all things, but when she experiences that the Beloved has stolen her heart, it seems he leaves her helpless instead of transforming her in total loving union. 3. The wounds of love are wonderful for the soul, but she suffers from the fact the love is incomplete and cannot fully satisfy. The longing for complete union is painful and the soul will never be satisfied except in total love.

> Extinguish these miseries,
> since no one else can stamp them out
> and may my eyes behold you,
> because you are their light,
> and I would open them to you alone.

Commentary: 4. She asks her Beloved to satisfy her longings with the vision of his presence. 5. Only pure love can bring fulfillment. All else are weary and annoying distractions—miseries only overcome with the refreshing presence of the Beloved. 6. The Beloved wants to satisfy the soul's longings once she has abandoned all desire for consolation and satisfaction in anything but the love of the Beloved. 7 God comes when the soul is thus exclusively focused on God. 8. The soul reminds God that she has no love except for God alone and the illuminating vision of divine presence. 9. The soul seeks to persuade the Bridegroom that all is darkness except the light he brings to her life.

Stanza 11.

Introduction: 1. God grants an awareness of divine presence to the soul who relentlessly pursues God, a revelation of divine beauty. This communication intensifies the soul's desire for deeper union, and as the longing increases so God's gifts of glimpses of divine presence enflame the soul's longings of love.

> Reveal your presence,
> and may the vision of your beauty be my death;
> for the sickness of love
> is not cured
> except by your presence and image.

Commentary: 2. Desiring to possess God more deeply, the soul asks God to reveal the divine essence which is beauty, even if this means an end to earthly life, for her longing of love can find no cure except in the vision of God. 3. God is present to a soul in three ways: first, as creator—God sustains all in existence; second, God offers a transforming presence to those in grace; third, God is spiritually present in love for souls who long for God. Each of these remains partial in this life. 4. Here the soul asks God to reveal the divine self in affective union which gives her glimpses of the divine beauty which generally lies hidden. As she glimpses this loving presence she longs for more, feels pained with intense desire, and is drawn to the presence and to nothing else. 5. However, the soul realizes that for a human to see God would mean death. 6. Thus, she acknowledges that she could not endure this revelation of divine presence and yet she says if it needs to include death, let it be so. 7. The soul who has seen glimpses of God's loving presence would be willing to die in order to share in this vision again. 8. The soul accepts death because she is convinced she cannot see God without dying. Corruptible human life is incompatible with the incorruptible life of God. 9-10. In earlier times people feared God, but with Christ's coming and his revelation of God's love, people can now long to see God. Death is no longer reason to fear but to rejoice in the opportunity to see God and to be transformed into the very beauty of God. The person who loves, does not fear death but desires it, for he or she appreciates that it takes away all evil. 11. Love-sickness has no remedy except the presence of the Beloved. God is health for the love-sick soul; the more love increases the healthier the soul will be. 12. In the perfection of love the lover is transformed into the Beloved, then her health is complete. 13. Imperfect love is like a sickness leaving the soul too weak to practice heroic virtues. 14. However, when one feels this sickness it means the person definitely has some love. Without this sickness, a person has no love or perfect love.

Stanza 12.

Introduction: 1. The soul feels she is rushing to God and that God is completing the work of her transformation. She glimpses God's beauty and receives God's love.

> O spring like crystal!
> If only, on your silvered-over faces,
> you would suddenly form
> the eyes I have desired,
> which I bear sketched deep within my heart.

Commentary: 2. The soul ardently longs for union, cannot find it in creatures, and realizes she must seek the union in the truth of faith. Thus, she asks that God uncover the obscurity of faith and manifest the divine presence. 3. Faith is like a crystal spring, clear and pure, watering the soul. It is the gift of the Spirit. 4. If the truth and substance of faith is like gold, then the propositions of faith are like silver. The latter we believe now, the former we will enjoy in eternity. Faith requires us to close the eyes of the intellect but when faith comes to an end we will possess the clear vision of God. Nevertheless, faith communicates God to us truly, even though covered with the restrictions of this life. 5. So, the soul is asking that God reveal explicitly without restrictions those truths hidden in articles of faith. 6. These truths of faith are infused in the soul, intellect, and will, even though an imperfect sketch that later will become a finished painting. 7. This sketch of faith is completed by the vision of love when the lover becomes like the Beloved in total union and transformation. 8. Then the soul can say with St. Paul that she no longer lives, but that it is Christ who lives in her. The lives of both become one in the transforming union of love, anticipated in this life and completed in the next. Although this life's union is only a sketch in comparison to the transformation in glory, it is still a wonderful blessing—a spiritual marriage. 9. Even in this life the soul's experience is indescribable. The soul thirsts for God and the intensity of her longing is painful. She feels so near and yet not there, so close to the love she seeks, and yet deprived of it.

PART II

Stanza 13.

Introduction: 1. The soul suffers a lot at this time since she feels deeply the pain of the absence of the love she has touched and now longs for. She feels intolerable darkness even when God is spiritually near—unable to see because of the excessive light. The closer the soul comes to God but is not totally transformed in love, the more she feels emptiness and darkness until she is transformed. As the soul accepts the darkness and emptiness, God favors her with consolation and love. In her painful purification God supports her with love.

> Withdraw them, Beloved,
> I am taking flight!
> Return, dove,
> the wounded stag
> is in sight on the hill,
> cooled by the breeze of your flight.

Commentary: 2. The Beloved grants his strong love to the soul in proportion to the intensity of her yearnings and the depth of her love. At times this becomes too much for anyone, and she feels outside of self—her weak humanity unable to endure the inbreak of God's purifying and transforming love. She feels outside of her own body and that is where she longs to be in order to be united with her Beloved. However, the Bridegroom impedes this flight, insisting that the lover live and love in this present life for he longs for her love as she does for his. 3. As the soul receives interior communication and knowledge she realizes her human nature is too weak and she must ask that the Beloved withdraw. 4. So, these loving visits torment and endanger her human weakness. God protects her, otherwise she would die. When the Spirit communicates with the soul God raises up the soul seemingly outside the body. This rupture of one's total self produces intense pain, so unbearable that the soul asks the Beloved to withdraw. 5. While she asks him to withdraw she really doesn't want him to do so, but she is afraid. She enjoys the Beloved's presence and wants it to continue, but she cannot receive him fully in this body and pleads that he withdraw her to the life of the spirit when she can enjoy the union for which she longs. 6. So, the soul takes flight from her body to be able in the spirit to unite herself with the Beloved. The soul feels she is carried away outside her bodily self in a form of rapture. In earlier stages of the spiritual life she would feel the pain of this break, and the pain itself would bring her back to life in the body. In this stage of union the soul receives these special communications in gentleness, peace, and love, and her bodily life is in no way disturbed by this union. 7. John points out it would be good to digress here to speak of the various kinds of raptures and ecstasies, but he doesn't have the time! Instead he suggests readers check the writings of Teresa of Avila. 8. The soul took flight from her body into spiritual union and thought her life was at an end, and she ready for total spiritual union. The Bridegroom had other ideas and told her to return from her pursuit of total union for the time is not yet. Rather, she should simply accept the communications she is already receiving. 9. Among lovers if one is wounded the other suffers too. Here the Bridegroom acknowledges the wound and suffering of the love-sick bride and asks her to return, otherwise he too will be in pain. 10. The knowledge and love the Bridegroom gives the bride is profound but not total. In contemplation God gives glimpses of the divine self—the soul catches sight of God. 11. Contemplation received from the Holy Spirit in this ecstasy causes a spirit of love in the soul. Knowledge leads to love and God communicates not in the knowledge but through the love. 12. God's gift of love refreshes the soul on fire with love, and causes that love to deepen. God gives this transforming love in proportion to the soul's unfailing love.

Stanzas 14 and 15.

Introduction: 1. The Bridegroom calls the bride to return to him, and she finds everything she wants in union with her Bridegroom. She sings his praises for all the grandeur of her Beloved which she enjoys and expresses in this union.

> My Beloved , the mountains,
> and lonely wooded valleys,
> strange islands,
> and resounding rivers,
> the whistling of love-stirring breezes,
>
> the tranquil night
> at the time of the rising dawn,
> silent music,
> sounding solitude,
> the supper that refreshes, and deepens love.

2. The bride has reached a high level of union in love—spiritual betrothal with the Son of God. When God first grants this union, God also communicates wonderful knowledge about divine life and grants extraordinary gifts to the soul. The resulting state of peace and enjoyment brings an end to the bride's intense and painful longings and her sense of unfulfilled love. She now describes her sense of peace and gentle love in these verses as she celebrates many good things about her Beloved. So, she no longer speaks of sufferings and longings but of the communication and peaceful love she feels in this spiritual betrothal. These two stanzas describe the fullness of the blessings God grants at this time, but not everyone receives all nor do they receive in the same intensity.

Commentary: 3. There are many mansions in the Father's house filled with blessings for the soul to enjoy. 4. Among these blessings the soul enjoys peaceful rest, understands secret knowledge of God, and experiences God's awesome power. Moreover, she enjoys the gratifying sense of true quiet and the illumination of the wisdom of God in the harmony of creation. She now feels filled with blessings and empty of evils. Above all she enjoys the refreshment of divine love which confirms her own love. 5 The bride experiences that everything God is in the essence of divinity; God is also this specifically for her. She experiences all the attributes of God personally and vitally. It isn't that the soul has a clear vision of the essence of God, but rather the overwhelming communication she feels is a glimpse into divine life and a profound awareness of the personal transforming presence of God in her life. She feels that everything God is in the divine essence God is all this for her alone. 6. As mountains are high, vast, beautiful, bright, and fragrant, so is God for the soul. 7. As wooded valleys offer pleasant shade, refreshment, opportunities for recreation, delight, solitude, and silence, so is the Beloved for the soul. 8. As strange islands offer seclusion and mysterious experiences, so God blesses the soul with wonderful new knowledge. As our experiences on strange islands are different than we are accustomed to, so the soul discovers God's ways are different than expected and wonderful to discover. 9. As powerful rivers inundate the land, fill in empty areas, and sound so loud as they rush by, so too, God floods upon the soul, fills all the voids in life, and is so overwhelming, the soul cannot hear anything else. 10. God's spirit is such a powerful force it overwhelms all else and the soul is possessed by it. This happened to the apostles at Pentecost and to Jesus in Gethsemane. This powerful voice of God is heard within the soul and bestows strength and fullness of blessings. 11. This voice of great power is not harsh and painful but gentle. God measures this communication of such a powerful force according to the capacity of each one, so that it always brings a sense of both delight and grandeur. 12. The whistling of love-stirring breezes refers to God's loving communication of the divine self in the soul's personal experience of God's attributes. This is one of God's most delightful communications. 13. As whistling breezes delight both a sense of touch and hearing, the soul enjoys a feeling of refreshment in the depths of her spirit and hears the communication of new knowledge in the vital experiences of God's attributes. 14. The delight the soul experiences fills her with a desire for union spurred on by God's loving communication of divine attributes—a subtle and delicate knowledge that penetrates to the depths of the soul. The soul receives this knowledge passively. 15. This communication of truths about the divinity and revelation of God's secrets is a manifestation, or spiritual revelation, or vision, which is given to the spirit without any aid of the senses. It is a vision received passively by the intellect. 16. Although this is a direct passive communication without any accidents, it still is dark for it comes in contemplation. The senses could not endure it. 17-20. The rapture and betrothal to which these verses refer causes fear and trembling in the soul because this communication of God' spirit is unendurable to human nature. Moving from natural ignorance and inability to supernatural knowledge causes fear and trembling in the soul even though this is not the essential vision of God. 21-23. The communication is gentle and not accompanied by fear and torment, except at the beginning. Rather, now the soul possesses peace and tranquility accompanied by a profound and obscure divine knowledge. The soul says her Beloved is like a tranquil night to her; so the obscure knowledge is not a dark night. Rather, this new knowledge is like a rising dawn that dispels darkness. In other words, the soul is raised from the darkness of natural knowledge to the light of a supernatural knowledge of God. As daybreak is not yet clear light, so too, this experience contains some obscurity while leading to new light and illumination. 24. The intellect is aware of being raised to divine light above all previous understanding. The soul is now in the highest level of contemplation, immerses herself in God's loving Spirit, enjoys being alone with God—stripped of all other interests—gives constant love-filled praise to God, and has no interest in sense-like satisfactions. 25. In this new illumination the soul becomes aware of the wonderful harmony God has placed in creation, so that it becomes a beautiful yet silent symphony revealing a likeness of God. 26. This revelation is heard alone by the spiritual faculties without natural forms or sounds. All creation silently makes common music, giving glory and praise to God. 27. The soul appreciates that every creature in its own way gives glory and praise to God, for something of the divine love is present in everything God has made. She now knows that every creature gives witness to God—this is a wonderful knowledge she has been given. 28. The knowledge nourishes, refreshes, and deepens love. This tranquil knowledge brings an end to the evils the soul experienced and leads her to the possession of good things. All this causes a deepening of her love for God. 29. In this union, God shares love with the soul in an enriching union. In fact, God becomes the soul's nourishment, refreshment, and deeper love. 30. What has been said in this section about spiritual betrothal means the soul enjoys complete tranquility and the most abundant communication possible in this stage in life. This is felt only in the spiritual part of the soul. The sensory part never completely loses its negative impact until the state of spiritual marriage. Betrothal includes visits of the Beloved who still withdraws at times leaving the bride in pain. Moreover, the sensory part still disturbs and afflicts the soul as does the power of evil. These negative traits cease in spiritual marriage.

Stanza 16.

Introduction: 1. The bride is filled with virtues and enjoys the visits of the Beloved who is delighted to see the bride's virtues. While the bride offers her virtues to the Beloved, he is delighted to receive them and enriches them with his gifts. The soul feels the Bridegroom is deep within her. She offers herself to him and finds this gift of herself is one of the greatest services she performs for her Beloved, and this union delights her. 2. The powers of evil seek to disrupt this peaceful joy. The soul has gained much and has much to lose. Although the soul's sensory appetites are now deadened, nevertheless, evil seeks to stir up these appetites, undesireable images, sensory movements, and even disturbances in the spiritual part too. When these things happen the soul cannot free herself from them without God's interventions to restore peace.

> Catch us the foxes,
> for our vineyard is now in flower,
> while we fashion a cone of roses
> intricate as the pine's;
> and let no one appear on the hill.

Commentary: 3. The bride prays that all these disturbances be blocked so that they cannot interfere with the union in love. 4. When the bride unites her will with the wishes of the Bridegroom her virtues flourish, and must continue in spite of the disturbances that can arise. 5. Appetites and sensory powers seem to be asleep but rise up when the bride grows in union and virtue. Then they arise to thwart and contradict this loving growth, and to stimulate the flesh against the spirit. 6. The soul faces two threats: these negative appetites wage war on the peaceful growth of the soul, and bodily torments and spiritual horrors afflict her. These sometimes happen before the soul is appropriately fortified in the spiritual growth, thus attempting to block the growth before it happens. Once she attains growth she can recollect herself in spirit against these disturbances. 7. The soul prays that both she and her Beloved, united in the flowering of virtue, be protected from these onslaughts. 8. At this time the soul sometimes sees her own virtues and rejoices, recognizing they are hers and gifts from God and she offers each and all in love to her Beloved, finding he is present with her in this gift. 9. This gift of virtues is made up of perfect, strong, and rich gifts, making up the perfection of the soul which she offers to her Beloved. 10. The bride also asks for solitude and withdrawal from all natural knowledge and appetites that can pray on the integrity of her self-gift, distracting her concentration. 11. The soul needs this to enjoy the communion with God. When appetites are active they hinder this communion. Later, when the soul reaches deeper union these distractions will disappear. For now she prays for total focus of the will on union with her Beloved.

Stanza 17.

Introduction: 1. The soul enjoys so much her union with the Beloved that when he is absent she feels intense pain. As her love becomes more intense, so too does she feel intense pain in absence. At the same time she finds any disturbance from creatures to be a very painful distraction from concentrating on the one thing she wants—union with God. Since she has tasted the joy of union she appreciates what is missing when it is not there and fears even momentary absence.

> Be still, deadening north wind;
> south wind come, you that waken love,
> breathe through my garden,
> let its fragrance flow,
> and the Beloved will feed amid the flowers.

Commentary: 2. Spiritual dryness is also a threat to the soul's maintenance of union. She attempts to limit its influence through prayer and through petitioning the work of the Holy Spirit to dispel the dryness and increase the practice of virtue and the pursuit of love. 3. Spiritual dryness is like a deadening north wind that stunts the growth of virtue and love but the soul can only react with the aid of her Bridegroom. 4. The Holy Spirit awakens her love, refreshes her spirit, and elevates the will to the love of God. 5. The Holy Spirit also brings to life the soul's virtues, renewing and perfecting them. 6. Sometimes the Holy Spirit reveals to the soul all the beauty of her virtues all together or individually, and she rejoices to see the wonders of God in her. 7. Often the soul reacts to this revelation with such joy that it overflows from her inner spirit, and others can recognize in her the delight of this special experience and they remain awestruck. 8. The Son of God is communicated to the soul in these visits of the Holy Spirit. The Spirit prepares the bride by showing forth her gifts and virtues, by controlling the effects of appetites, by opening herself to the transformation of the Spirit, and by intensifying the practice of virtues. In this way she gains enjoyment in her Beloved and he in her. This continues as long as the Bridegroom sustains her. 9. Each one should long for this transforming presence of the Holy Spirit, not for self-satisfaction but to the please the Beloved. 10. At this time the Son takes delight in her, he nourishes and sustains her, and he dwells within her because she pleases him. He communicates himself to her, transforming her into himself and he too feels nourished by her love.

Stanza 18.

Introduction: 1. In this state of spiritual betrothal the soul sees and appreciates her own gifts and goodness and knows her union with her Beloved is incomplete as long as she dwells in her body. She suffers intensely, feeling imprisoned in her body and from time to time must deal with bad appetites, inordinate movements, and sensory rebellions that threaten the peaceful union she has attained.

> You girls of Judea,
> while among flowers and roses
> the amber spreads its perfume,
> stay away, there on the outskirts:
> do not so much as seek to touch our thresholds.

Commentary: 3. The soul desires to preserve her state of union and growth in virtue, and she prays that all sensory temptations be still and not disquiet her peaceful union. 4. These lower faculties and appetites strive to attract both the will and the intellect to pursue the object of their temptations, away from the interior and spiritual to the exterior and carnal. 5. Rather, the soul wants to focus on virtues and on the spiritual faculties—memory, intellect, and will, for these can maintain her union in love. 6. When this is her focus, then the Bridegroom's divine Spirit abides in her. 7. The soul prays that all distracting images stay away and the sensory part be stilled. She knows that the interior spirit can be distracted by the sensory part through the exterior senses and also through the interior senses. She prays they all stay away and not even cross the threshold into her soul.

Stanza 19.

Introduction: 1. The soul desires the most perfect communication of God and knows this is always restricted when the sensory part is involved, and so she prays that God allows no communication to the lower part but only to the spiritual.

Hide yourself, my love;
turn your face toward the mountains,
and do not speak;
but look at those companions
going with her through strange islands.

Commentary: 2. The bride asks four things of the Bridegroom: that he communicate inwardly in the hiding place of the soul, that he inform her higher faculties with knowledge of God, that this communication be ineffable and away from the sensory part, and that he be pleased with her life of virtue. 3. She prays that her Beloved withdraw to the innermost part of her soul and communicate in secret. 4. She also prays that divinity give the intellect divine knowledge, impart divine love to the will, and take possession of the memory. She no longer wants indirect communication but the essential communication of the divinity. 5. Thus, she desires no communication through the senses but rather communication that is imperceptible to senses within the deepest recesses of the soul. 6. She asks God to look at her virtues and spiritual gifts and be pleased with the transformation God's gifts have wrought in her soul. God is pleased with these gifts in the soul and lovingly transforms them even more. 7. The soul realizes that she receives strange knowledge that is foreign to the senses and prays that God's communication be interior and sublime.

Stanzas 20 and 21.

Introduction: 1. At this point in her journey the soul yearns for spiritual marriage which requires complete purification of all imperfections, the subjection of the lower faculties to the higher, and a singular and courageous love. In this new stage of union the soul receives profound purity, beauty, and strength. 2. To reach this stage requires purity, fortitude, and love. The Holy Spirit effects this union and desires that the soul possess all the heroic virtues that lead to the lofty love of spiritual marriage and that her will be totally concentrated on the true "yes" of love. 3. The soul desiring this perfect union says she is strong, her love lofty, and her virtues profound. The Bridegroom pledges to complete the soul's purification and to strengthen and prepare her sensory and spiritual parts for this new state of spiritual marriage.

> Swift-winged birds,
> lions, stags, and leaping roes,
> mountains, lowlands, and river banks,
> waters, winds, and ardors,
> watching fears of night:

> By the pleasant lyres,
> and the siren's song, I conjure you
> to cease your anger
> and not touch the wall,
> that the bride may sleep in deeper peace.

Commentary: 4. The Bridegroom gives the bride peace and tranquility by conforming all aspects of the lower part to the higher. He controls the wanderings of the phantasy and imagination, brings anger and concupiscence under the control of reason, perfects the direction of the spiritual faculties of intellect, memory, and will, and controls the four passions of joy, hope, fear, and sorrow. Thus, the whole self is directed to God and spiritual values. 5. When the soul's will is focused on enjoyment of the Beloved the wanderings of imagination interrupt this communication. The Bridegroom blocks these digressions. 6. Impetuosity and concupiscence lead to false boldness and daring, and to cowardice in face of difficulties. 7. The Beloved bridles the anger and impetuosity, strengthens against cowardice, and focuses the intense desire on satisfaction in him alone. Anger and concupiscence do not cease, but the Beloved controls their disturbing and inordinate actions. 8. The acts of the three spiritual faculties of memory, intellect, and will can become inordinate when either too high in presumption, too low in cowardliness, or frustrated in attaining their goal—as in excess, defect, or imbalanced focus. Again the Beloved leads the soul to a just balance without extremes. 9. The four passions of sorrow, hope, joy, and fear that afflict the soul, yearn for the wrong object, inflame the heart, and hinder good; all disturb the soul's peacefulness. 10. The Beloved brings an end to these passions' negative effects on the soul. Thus, he removes the soul's sorrow even over past sins and while the soul knows what causes sorrow she no longer feels it. 11. Experiencing the fullness of joy in God's presence the soul is completely satisfied and has no further hopes, no other longings. 12. Likewise, having complete joy she is not distracted by other joys. If new joys come, even spiritual, she turns instead to the fullness of joy she already has. 13. She no longer needs new joys for she can always enjoy anew the satisfaction she already has. 14. The Beloved bestows on his bride the gift of enjoying even more deeply what he has already given to her. 15. She is so illumined and strong that she rests in union with her Beloved, freed of the negative affects of the passions. She rests in God's peace. 16-19. So, the Beloved brings an end to previous disturbances, bitterness, and sorrow, and leads the soul to refreshment, as in a protected garden where she enjoys the sleep of love.

PART III

Stanza 22.

Introduction: 1. During the journey so far, the Bridegroom has been working all the time to free his bride from evil tendencies, and he rejoices that she is now liberated.

The bride has entered
the sweet garden of her desire,
and she rests in delight,
laying her neck
on the gentle arms of her Beloved.

Commentary: 2. The bride has sought to control all lower appetites and has also sought the Holy Spirit to dispel dryness and to increase love. The Bridegroom tells her how she has reached this stage of spiritual marriage and what rewards she can now enjoy. 3. This present stage of spiritual marriage is a total transformation in the Beloved and is much greater than spiritual betrothal. Here each surrenders self to the other in a union of love in which the soul participates in divine life. This is the highest state attainable in this life and implies a confirmation in grace. The Beloved and the bride become one. 4. The bride enters a new level of existence, leaving aside all former ways whether temporal, natural, or spiritual. Now, she has reached full transformation in spiritual marriage, a state beyond words and thoughts. Even this cannot be perfect in this life. 5. Prior to this state of spiritual marriage the bride surrenders herself in love to the Bridegroom who now communicates delights and grandeurs to her. The bride's aim is now focused on the fullness of this state in which she finds secure and stable peace beyond the growth of spiritual betrothal. She now lives in her Bridegroom's embrace, totally transformed in him. 6. She rests in union with her Bridegroom who becomes her strength, protecting her from all evil and subduing all appetites and passion. He is also her delight in direct union.

Stanza 23.

Introduction: 1. In this high state of spiritual marriage the Bridegroom reveals wonderful secrets to the soul as to a faithful consort, including deeper understanding of the mysteries of the Incarnation and Redemption.

> Beneath the apple tree:
> there I took you for my own,
> there I offered you my hand,
> and restored you,
> where your mother was corrupted.

Commentary: 2. The Bridegroom explains how he redeemed his bride from the corruption of sin by his passion and death on the cross and restored humanity to God's favor and mercy. 3. The Son redeemed humanity by his death and then pledged to each one his grace to reach spiritual espousal. 4. Thus, he raised up the bride from her lowly stage to become his companion and spouse. 5. God drew good from evil, redemption from a tree, as formerly all was lost under a tree. 6. God espoused each one of us once and for all by the grace of the cross. But the espousal we speak of in this stage of the spiritual journey is achieved only gradually. God takes us to divine life in a moment of redemptive grace, but we strive step by step to enter into union.

Stanza 24.

Introduction: 1 The bride reclines in loving union with the Bridegroom, enjoying the divine life of grace and beauty.

> Our bed is in flower,
> bound round with linking dens of lions,
> hung with purple,
> built up in peace,
> and crowned with a thousand shields of gold.

Commentary: 2. The bride enjoys the graces and grandeurs of the Beloved in peace and security and finds she is endowed with rich gifts and virtues and possesses them with fortitude. She feels she now has perfect love, spiritual peace, and delight in union. 3. Her Bridegroom communicates his wisdom, grace, virtues, and gifts which she and he enjoy together. 4. In union with her Bridegroom she feels protected and safe from evils. 5. Her many virtues reinforce each other, protecting her from disquiet, liberating her from disturbances of natural passions and temporal cares, and keeping her free from disturbances of her enemies of world, flesh, and devil. 6. Filled with the delights of God, in peace and tranquility, the bride is filled with perfect virtues which she enjoys, although not all the time. In this state she beholds the abundance, grandeur, and beauty of God with rest, refreshment, and protection. She receives strange knowledge of God, an awareness of God's greatness, and a celebration of divine gifts. 7. The soul receives such joy because of God's charity and love, and this enkindles her love of God, moving her with love to love God more. 8. A further excellence of this union is perfect peace of soul. The bride's virtues produce in her peace, meekness, and fortitude which make her strong against the onslaughts of the world, devil, and flesh. 9. The bride's virtues are her reward for her efforts to acquire them but become also her shield against vice and evil.

Stanza 25.

Introduction: 1. The soul is profoundly grateful not only for the gifts she has received from her Beloved but also for the many gifts he has poured out on others.

> Following your footprints
> maidens run along the way;
> the touch of a spark,
> the spiced wine,
> cause flowings in them from the balsam of God.

Commentary: 2. So, the bride praises her Bridegroom for three favors he gives to others to raise them in love of God. He grants them support to pursue perfection, inflames their love, and infuses an abundance of charity. 3. The bride sees these traces of God's love for others and recognizes the presence of her Bridegroom. 4. Thus strengthened, each one in his or her own way pursues spiritual perfection, or rather is drawn towards God. 5. These souls give themselves to external practices and good works but also increase the interior exercise of the will. These lead the Beloved to inflame these souls with love and enkindle their will in love, praise, gratitude, and reverence for God. 6. Thus the Beloved produces a touch of love in the soul, greater or lesser depending on the perfection of the soul, and the soul responds in desire, love, and praise of God. 7. God sometimes goes further and inebriates the soul with strong love, and she responds with increased praise, love, and reverence. 8. This inebriation lasts longer than the former touch of love and the soul knows deep down that God is inflaming her with love. The touch of love is like a spark, it passes quickly but its effect last longer since the soul is set on fire with love. The inebriation of love and its effects are equal to each other in length of time. 9. There is new love and old love, like new wine and old wine. New wine is still in process and one does not know its quality until the process is complete—it can even be harmful. Old wine is mature, the process complete, and its quality now evident—it is smooth, strengthens, and makes one feel good. 10. New lovers are beginners, their fervor sensory; still in process, they are motivated by the sensible satisfaction. One should not trust this love until these externals have passed. It can lead to more mature love, but its novelty can also lead to failure. Such new lovers become anxious in their love and should practice moderation until their love matures. 11. Old lovers have a mature love that they have perfected in the service of the Bridegroom. Their love is not based on sensible satisfaction but it is deep within their inner spirit and reflected in good works. Being above the need of sensory satisfaction and its afflictions, they no longer have anxieties of their love. Rather, they are faithful to God and above temptations of sensuality. God esteems this level of love and inebriates the soul with divine life, and the soul for her part directs all her love to God.

Stanza 26.

Introduction: 1. The soul now rests secure with her Bridegroom and feels the transforming presence of God deep within her spirit, overflowing with love.

> In the inner wine cellar
> I drank of my Beloved, and, when I went abroad
> through all this valley
> I no longer knew anything,
> and lost the herd which I was following.

Commentary: 2. The soul experiences the intimacy of God's love and is now withdrawn from all worldly things and finds all her appetites are now controlled. 3. The soul finds herself immersed in the most intimate degree of love possible in this life, beyond other steps of love that led her here. Now she has attained a level of love based on the seven gifts of the Holy Spirit. 4. Few people reach this last level of love which is spiritual marriage. It is an experience beyond words in which the soul is transformed in God in intimate union—wonderful but not as perfect as in the next life. 5. In this transformation God first communicates to the very substance and spiritual faculties of the soul, 6. secondly she receives divine wisdom, 7. and thirdly, God transforms her love into divine love. 8. While it is generally thought that love builds on knowledge, in this experience the soul is on fire with love without understanding—she understands little but loves much. God infuses love and increases charity without necessarily increasing knowledge of God. 9. Fourth, the memory is illumined by knowledge of former gifts of the Beloved. 10. So, this experience of love deifies, elevates, and immerses the soul in God. 11-12. Once drawn to this state of spiritual marriage the soul remains there even though her faculties are not always in actual union. The spiritual marriage is permanent, while actual union is not continuous. 13. In this transforming union the soul forgets all worldly things, informed instead with supernatural knowledge which makes all other knowledge seem as ignorance. 14. The soul raised up to God and immersed in love gives no attention to worldly issues nor to herself, but absorbed in love she has an unknowing to all else. God has destroyed the soul's imperfection, and she like Adam in the garden becomes ignorant and totally disinterested in all sin. 15. Immersed in God, the soul is drawn away from all interest in external affairs. 16. Normal acquired human knowledge and science remains, and is even perfected, but is overwhelmed by supernatural knowledge. 17. This absorption in love overwhelms all else, so the soul rarely actually thinks of other things and her focus is simple, contemplative insight, not imaginative issues. In this state of unknowing the soul cannot avert to anything in particular, especially old ways of knowing. Rather, her new kind of life is all love. 18. Some slight appetites and imperfections will always remain until the soul reaches this state of perfection in glory: the intellect still tries to know things in old ways; the will might still pursue former appetites, tastes, and desires; the memory can be disturbed by useless imaginings. 19. There still remain useless hopes, joys, sorrows, and fears, until these are transformed in love.

Stanza 27.

Introduction: 1. God communicates to the soul with extraordinary intimacy, tenderness, and humility, becoming servant to the soul. 2. Overwhelmed by such love, the soul completely surrenders herself to God, thus there develops a profound mutual surrender of God and the soul.

> There he gave me his breast;
> there he taught me a sweet and living knowledge;
> and I gave myself to him,
> keeping nothing back;
> there I promised to be his bride.

Commentary: 3-4. The bride describes this mutual surrender as total and the divine communication in which God teaches her as a secret wisdom. 5. God also teaches the soul love-filled mystical knowledge in contemplation that enriches both intellect and will. 6. Thus, God transforms the soul, purifying and perfecting her and making her totally given to God. In reply the soul gives herself totally to God— her will and all her actions in complete and permanent fidelity. 7. Now the soul's will, actions, cares, and appetites are all centered on God's will alone. All movements of faculties go first to God, nothing else is important. 8. So, the soul now only knows how to love and give self to God. She appreciates that nothing is important to her Beloved except love and that is what she wants to give, not only to please her Beloved but because his love within her motivates her to do just this. She has desire for nothing else.

Stanza 28.

Introduction: 1. God needs nothing that humans can give. However, God desires the soul's exaltation, and this is at its greatest when raised to the level of equality of love. She becomes bride, equal with her Beloved.

> Now I occupy my soul
> and all my energy in his service;
> I no longer tend the herd,
> nor have I any other work
> now that my every act is love.

Commentary: 2. The bride proves her total surrender in love by giving herself completely to the service of her Bridegroom, no longer seeking her own satisfaction in anything else. In dealing with God her only focus is love. 3. Her intellect, memory, and will are completely dedicated to God's service. 4. Even the energies of her sensory part she gives in service to God—all conformed to God's will (her four passions, natural appetites, and cares center only on God). 5. All these aspects of her life now naturally direct themselves to God even when the soul is unaware of it; 6. she no longer follows any other pleasure of desire; 7. and her former unprofitable occupations are laid aside now that her every act is love. 8. All she does is done for love; 9. and this total immersion in love delights God. 10. This is a happy state where the soul continually walks in union of love and with constant attentiveness to the will of God.

Stanza 29.

Introduction: 1. The soul has no interest in anything else except to love God and even withdraws from normal daily life to emphasize the one and only necessary thing—attentiveness to God and exercise of love. 2. Prior to this state the soul needed to practice love in both active and contemplative life, now she no longer wants to be involved in anything, even great works of service that could be a hindrance to an attentive love of God, which is the most precious gift a soul can make for herself and for the Church. 3. Directing a soul away from this pure love for any reason, even for good works, would be misdirected. Dedicated people who immerse themselves in activities would do well to re-establish the priority of loving union with God in prayer above all else. 4 So many criticize her soul's holy idleness, but she now knows the secret source of her fruitfulness is in love.

> If, then, I am no longer
> seen or found on the common,
> you will say that I am lost;
> That, stricken by love,
>   I lost myself, and was found.

Commentary: 5. The soul here responds to the reprimand others give her for her exclusive focus on the intimate love of God. Rather, she openly proclaims she has chosen well, leaving aside her former involvement to give herself totally to her Beloved. 6. She knows many people will think she has lost her way, 7. but she is not ashamed of the choices she has made; 8. she realizes that many people, given to good works never completely execute these works with complete detachment; 9. whereas she may seem lost, but she has found herself absorbed in love. 10. No one can serve two masters, and the soul claims she is willing to lose everything for love of God. She has left aside any interest in herself or in any creatures to surrender herself to God alone. 11. Losing every other interest to focus on love of God is a great gain. Losing herself, she gains her true self; she loses all that is not God and finds communion with God in faith and love.

Stanza 30.

Introduction: 1. The soul receives great delight from her union in love. The Bridegroom communicates himself and all his gifts to her bringing her consolation and happiness, and everything the bride possess brings gladness to the Bridegroom.

> With flowers and emeralds
> chosen on cool mornings
> we shall weave garlands
> flowering in your love,
> and bound with one hair of mine.

Commentary: 2. The bride describes the joy she finds in their mutual communion and love. She recognizes her virtues are gifts of the Bridegroom's love that they can both enjoy. 3. The soul's virtues and gifts, 4. acquired through strenuous opposition to vices in earlier life, 5. and matured through efforts in times of hardships and aridity, 6. are like a garland, all woven together as a perfect gift, making her worthy of her Beloved. She knows she cannot practice or acquire these virtues without God's help and yet she also knows her Bridegroom values her contribution—this is a work achieved together. 7. In many ways this is the work of the Church, gathering together the virtues of the faithful— virgins, doctors, and martyrs, all enriching the Church. 8. These virtues have value because of their love and because they come from God's love. 9. So too, the bride's love binds together her virtues and gifts, and without love the life of virtues would fall apart. For the bride, the simple focus of her will holds together her virtues—she desires nothing but love of God. Both God's love and the soul's love are necessary to preserve this life. 10-11. This life of virtue, blessed by God, brings beauty and strength to the soul, and keeps away all ugliness and imperfection.

Stanza 31.

Introduction: 1. The garland of interwoven virtues which describes the union between the bride and the Bridegroom also represents the Bridegroom himself to whom she is bound in love. The soul covered with the garland no longer appears as herself but as her lover. Even though substantially different, they seem so united as to be each other. 2. His union is truly wonderful. God, the great lover, absorbs the soul in divine life.

> You considered
> that one hair fluttering at my neck;
> you gazed at it upon my neck
> and it captivated you;
> and one of my eyes wounded you.

Commentary: 3. The love that binds them together is strong love. God appreciates the soul's love and loves her in return because of the purity and integrity of her faith. 4. The love that binds her virtues together is fortitude—persevering love—so that no contrary vice can break it. The Holy Spirit arouses this strong love, stirring the faculties to the exercise of love, and God deeply cherishes this. 5. God gazes appreciatively at this unique, exclusive, strong love, and loves the soul in return. 6. After years of efforts and purification of appetites, this love now stand out, detached, strong, unbreakable, and God further strengthens the binding together of this love and these virtues. 7. The soul has passed through many temptations and her love has been strengthened so much that God rewards her with divine union. 8. Although the soul's lowly life captures God's love, it is God who first transforms the soul by divine love. 9. The soul appeals to and captivates God because of her singular faith and fidelity, and God then wounds the soul with tender affection and love which draws her further into love. 10. The soul's union is in the intellect and the will, in faith and in love. The soul celebrates this union and thanks her Bridegroom, while also delighting that he is captivated by her love.

Stanza 32.

Introduction: 1. The power and tenacity of the soul's love of God binds God to her. She possesses God and God surrenders to her. It is love alone that motivates God in this way.

> When you looked at me
> your eyes imprinted your grace in me;
> for this you loved me ardently;
> and thus my eyes deserved
> to adore what they beheld in you.

Commentary: 2. Perfect love attributes all to the Beloved. The soul takes no credit for the love she now has, recognizing that this too is a gift, 3. For God looked on her with love, 4. mercifully infusing divine love in her. 5. So, she acknowledges that God gave her love and faith, making her worthy and capable of God's love. 6. God loves nothing outside of the divine self, so God loves the soul because she embodies God's own love. Love is the purpose of God's love. God loves the soul as part of the divine self. 7. So, the soul sees that it is God who has made her pleasing. 8. Although her faculties were previously fallen in their natural activities, they are now illumined and elevated by God's grace to see God in a new way and to appreciate the wonders of God's love. 9. A soul without this illumination fails to see God's love, or to serve God unceasingly, and is even unaware of God's transforming grace.

Stanza 33.

Introduction: 1. God's gaze of love cleanses, endows with grace, enriches, and illumines, thus removing all former ugliness from the soul and making the soul appealing to God. The soul should not forget her former sins so as to become presumptuous, but can always give thanks, and increase her confidence. 2. The bride rejoices in the mercies and dignity she has received with gratitude and love. Knowing she is unworthy and her transformation unmerited, she knows all is from God and boldly asks for continuation of the divine favors.

> Do not despise me;
> for if, before, you found me dark,
> now truly you can look at me
> since you have looked
> and left in me grace and beauty.

Commentary: 3. With courage the bride tells her beloved to no longer look down on her but rather esteem her because of his own gifts to her which have transformed her. 4. She does not declare this for selfish reasons but because of the loving gifts she has received. 5. She may have formerly been unsightly because of sin, 6 but is now worthy of the Bridegroom's attention because he can see his own gifts in her. 7. The Bridegroom seeing the bride endowed with grace, wants to give her more grace, appreciates her beauty, loves her for herself, communicates more love and grace, and is captivated by her love. 8. Thus, God exalts the soul that is pleasing, endowing her with more gifts, 9. so that she is worthy of esteem and of God's love.

Stanza 34.

Introduction: 1. This relationship of friendship and of indescribable love leads the soul to gratitude, and the Bridegroom to praise and to thank his bride. She looks at her former failings and unworthiness, and he looks at her transformed beauty and grace.

> The small white dove
> has returned to the ark with an olive branch;
> and now the turtledove
> has found its longed-for mate
> by the green river bands.

Commentary: 2. The Bridegroom sings of the bride's purity and appreciates how she has prepared herself for him. He insists that her former trials are over, and she can find good fortune, fulfillment, and refreshment in his love. 3. He expresses appreciation for her purity, simplicity, meekness, and contemplative love. 4. Like a dove, the soul has flown aimlessly in imperfection and sin but now comes to rest in the service of her Beloved, purified of former failures, victorious over her enemies, and at peace. 5. The bride formerly acted with restlessness, not finding what she longed for, but now she finds the union for which she has yearned. 6. Thus, her fatigues are now over, as she finds the fulfillment of all her desires. She rests in contemplative union, refreshed, protected, and deeply favored by her Beloved.

Stanza 35.

Introduction: 1. The Bridegroom celebrates the happiness of his bride who has now found peace in the love of her Bridegroom. She is now settled in God and God in her.

She has no other needs, and God communicates divine union to her in her solitude.

> She lived in solitude,
> and now in solitude has built her nest;
> and in solitude he guides her,
> he alone, who also bears
> in solitude the wound of love.

Commentary: 2. The Bridegroom does two things. He praises the bride's former withdrawal into solitude as a step to discovering and rejoicing in her Beloved. He also tells her that he loved her precisely because she withdrew from every other satisfaction and support in order to find true love in him. Thus, he now accepts her, feeds her, and guides her to God. 3. The soul that longs for God cannot find companionship anywhere except in God. 4. The bride wanted nothing to do with this world but strove for perfection in solitude and thus she attained refreshment and rest. 5. In this new found solitude the soul is alone in God. Having left aside all appetites and faculties, she now rediscovers her intellect centered on divine understanding, her will focused on love of God alone, and her memory filled with hope of divine knowledge. Emptied of inferior objects, her faculties now center on God. 6. In this experience of spiritual marriage God communicates directly to the soul without intermediaries, for he gives the divine self fully to her and wants her exclusive love. He is now her only guide, and he lovingly draws her to greater favors. 7. The Bridegroom is wounded with love for the bride and wounded by her love for him. He joins her in her solitude, guides her, and absorbs her in himself.

PART IV

Stanza 36.

Introduction: 1. Love is a union between two alone, and just like lovers like to be alone in their companionship, so too the bride and her Bridegroom no longer have any other activity except the joy of their intimate love and want no other distractions. 2. As the bride and Bridegroom enjoy each other's company, there is nothing left for them except the perfect enjoyment of God in eternal life.

> Let us rejoice, Beloved,
> and let us go forth to behold ourselves in your beauty
> to the mountain and to the hill
> to where the pure water flows,
> and further, deep into the thicket.

Commentary: 3. Enjoying the perfect union of love, the bride asks three things of her Bridegroom: to receive and savor the joy of love; to become like the Beloved in his beauty; and to know even deeper secrets of the Beloved. 4. She rejoices in the communication of love but also wants it to overflow into effective and actual practice of love and in exterior works directed to the service of the Beloved; so love expresses itself in contemplative union and in action. 5. She asks that by means of this double exercise of love they may both attain the vision of themselves in the beauty of the Bridegroom. 6. This means going to the mountain of God and together gaining a touch of the essential knowledge of God; to experience God's wisdom in the divine Word, in the creatures, works, and wonders of the world. 7. So, the bride is asking that she be transformed into the beauty of divine wisdom and resemble the Word, the Son of God, while also knowing the lesser wisdom contained in creatures. 8. When transformed into the wisdom of God the soul will then be able to see herself in the beauty of God. 9. God bestows this knowledge and wisdom on the intellect, contemplatively, cleansed of images and accidents. The more the soul loves, the more she wants to enter into this fuller experience of truths of divine life. 10. God's wisdom and knowledge is so deep and immense that there is always more for the soul to discover and she longs to do so. 11. The intensity of the soul's longing to penetrate more deeply into this knowledge of God is so profound she will pay any price, even the agony of death. 12. Suffering is the means for her to penetrate more deeply into this dense forest of the knowledge of God. Suffering in love leads to intimate knowledge and resulting joy. 13. A soul cannot reach this depth of intimacy without suffering, for the gate to this wisdom is the cross. In this suffering the soul finds delight and consolation for she knows it is the way to deeper union.

Stanza 37.

Introduction: 1. One of the main reasons the soul has for seeing this life come to an end is in order to be with God and to understand the profound mysteries of the Incarnation and of the ways of God.

> And then we will go on
> to the high caverns in the rock
> which are so well concealed;
> there we shall enter
> and taste the fresh juice of the pomegranates.

Commentary: 2. The soul longs to enter into this deep union with God—which is spiritual marriage—in order to unite her intellect with God in the knowledge of the mysteries of the Incarnation. The bride and the Bridegroom immerse themselves together into these mysteries and vitally experience the attributes of God. 3. The soul experiences the revelation of the hidden mysteries of God; the Incarnation, the harmony of God's justice and mercy, the history of salvation, God's secret judgments and foreknowledge, and so on. 4. Even though Church doctors have taught us so much, there is still more to be discovered. The soul can discover these mysteries once she has passed through purifying sufferings to divine wisdom, matured spiritually, and received many favors from God. 5. The soul enters these hidden places of revelation of the mysteries of God and is transformed and inebriated in the love of her Beloved. 6. Since the soul and God are now united in spiritual marriage they enter into this profound revelation together, for the soul is so absorbed in God that she does nothing on her own any more. As she enters into these mysteries she is further transformed in the love of God. With unspeakable delight she thanks and praises the Father through the Son. 7. The attributes, mysteries, judgment, and virtues of God are marvelously and wonderfully revealed. 8. As the bride and Bridegroom together experience the overflowing knowledge of God's attributes, infused wonders, and grandeurs, they delight in the deeper fruition of love, which is the gift of the Holy Spirit.

Stanza 38.

Introduction: 1. So, the bride celebrates that the bridegroom transforms her into the beauty of God, immersed in the understanding of the mysteries of God, of created and uncreated wisdom. She delights in these experiences and gives glory to her Bridegroom.

> There you will show me
> what my soul has been seeking,
> and then you will give me,
> you, my life, will give me there
> what you gave me on that other day.

Commentary: 2. The soul has always longed for this union of love; namely to love God as perfectly as God has loved her. She asks her Bridegroom to show her how to love in this way, thus she will receive the glory destined for her for all eternity. 3. Lovers always want to love as much as they are loved, and so the soul wanting this and yet knowing it is not possible in this life, longs for the excellence and power of love that only comes in glory. In this final transformation the soul's intellect, will, and love become God's. Now there is only one intellect, will, and love which is God's. However, even now in this state of spiritual marriage, the soul understands, wills, and loves through the gift of the Holy Spirit. 4. The soul prays that God will show her how to love as perfectly as she desires; to love purely, freely, disinterestedly, and with strength as God loves her. God transforms her into divine love and gives her divine strength in her love. Again we repeat that this is for the next life, but even now in spiritual marriage there is a living and totally ineffable semblance of that love. 5. God promises the soul eternal glory in the vision of God. While seeing God is the end, the soul stresses the surrender of herself in love for God. Perfect love requires the perfect vision of God. 6. God has predestined the soul to this ineffable vision from all eternity and nothing can take it away from her. 7. This experience is indescribable and Scripture uses various suggestive images to indicate what it is—tree of life, paradise, crown, hidden manna, power, white garment, the book of life. 8-9. It is an experience of unmistakable majesty and grandeur, and all descriptions fall short of the reality. However, what God predestined the soul to, he now gives on the day of spiritual marriage as he transforms his bride.

Stanza 39.

Introduction: 1. As the bride feels within herself something of this transformation, she struggles to attempt to explain a little of this vision.

> The breathing of the air,
> the song of the sweet nightingale,
> the grove and its living beauty
> in the serene night
> with a flame that is consuming and painless.

Commentary: 2. So, the bride calls this vision the breath of the Holy Spirit from her to God and from God to her. She says it is jubilation in the enjoyment of God. It is the appreciation of creatures and their orderly arrangement in the plan of God. It is a pure contemplation of the divine essence. And it is a total transformation in the immense love of God. 3. The Holy Spirit raises up the soul and makes her capable of breathing the new life of God; thus she is transformed into the life of the Trinity. Thus transformed into the life of God, the soul can breathe forth to God God's own life of love. 4. This transformation and mutual sharing of spirit to Spirit happens frequently although not as much as in the next life. It is a form of deification as the soul becomes God through participation, and she now understands, knows, and loves in the Trinity, together with the Trinity, as the Trinity itself. Transformed in God's power, wisdom, and love, the soul is like God; made in God's own image and likeness. 5. We cannot understand how this happens except to realize that the Son of God attained this for us. Thus, the Father gives to the soul the same love he showed to the Son, precisely because the Son asked that this be done. 6. Now the soul possesses by participation what the Son has by nature. This happens in the next life, but here, too, as a foretaste. 7. How sad it is that so many souls are unaware of their destiny. 8. The soul knows she is now free from all temporal disturbances, hears the voice of her Bridegroom, and experiences this transformation, and she expresses to him her jubilation. 9. She is refreshed in seeing the end of evil and the beginning of transformed life and praises God together with God now present in her. 10. Yet in her rejoicing, the soul is also aware that her song is not as perfect as it will be in the next life. 11. This vision also includes the appreciation of the living beauty of creation and of how all creatures are rooted and live in God, the Creator. The soul unites herself with this beauty and harmony as part of her self-gift to and with God. 12. The soul beholds all this in the night of contemplation, in which God teaches the soul passively, wordlessly, through a new knowing which is unknowing. 13. This contemplation is still a dark night in comparison to the knowledge in the life of glory, and here the soul asks for this clear and serene contemplation of the vision of God. 14. She knows this can only be brought to completion through the love of the Holy Spirit which transforms the soul in God and does so painlessly in the next life. In this life transformation through love is painful, but in this eternal vision there is no pain. 15. The bride longs for this final communication and knows that it requires of her the strongest and highest love. So she asks that this knowledge be communicated to her in consummated, perfect, and strong love.

Stanza 40.

No one looked at her,
nor did Aminadab appear;
the siege was still;
and the cavalry,
at the sight of the waters, descended.

Introduction and Commentary: 1. The bride knows that her entire being is now in harmony with the spirit; she has overcome all rebelliousness and is united and transformed in God. She asks her Bridegroom to confirm these blessings; that her soul be totally detached from all things, that evil be conquered, that passions and appetites be subjected, that all the sensory part be brought in conformity with the spiritual. 2. She states she has no further interest in anything except delight in her Bridegroom. 3. Her life is now so favored, strong, and filled with virtue that the devil has no further power over her. 4. All former attacks by passions and appetites are now over. 5. In this state of spiritual marriage even sensory faculties and natural strengths now share in the joys of the spirit. 6. While the sensory part cannot in this life naturally enjoy life of the spirit, it can receive refreshment and delight from a spiritual overflow that draws sense to appreciate the inner recollection. 7. The bride sets all this before her Bridegroom, asking that he continue these blessings, but more particularly that he transfer her from this spiritual marriage to the glorious marriage of the next life.

CHAPTER FIVE

THE DYNAMISM OF THE SPIRITUAL LIFE IN THE SPIRITUAL CANTICLE

Introduction

John insists that the *Spiritual Canticle* deals with the whole of the spiritual journey from the soul's early service of God to the stage of spiritual marriage (see C. Theme.1-2). The *Spiritual Canticle* presents a series of steps in the union of love and describes a process from a heart that is enslaved to false values and false ways of loving, to a liberated heart that centers all on God and knows how to love. As in his other works, John follows the traditional view of the spiritual life as divided into the purgative way of beginners (C. 1-5), the illuminative way of the proficient (C. 6-12), and the unitive way of the perfect (C. 13-40). The latter stage is divided into the two phases of union, namely spiritual betrothal (C. 13-21) and spiritual marriage (C. 22-40). The focal point of the journey is always love, and even in the early stages of purification we are always dealing with the deep yearnings of a lover: "Where have you hidden Beloved"; with one who already knows the Beloved: "Him I love most, tell him I am sick, I suffer, and I die." We have seen that John writes his poem to portray the dynamic attitudes of the one who pursues deeper love. Thus, the two parts of preparation (C. 1-5 and C. 6-12) encourage a sense of urgency in the reader. There are no adjectives or adverbs in these sections, and both the poem and its teachings move urgently and rapidly to union. However, once he arrives at the two stages of union he urges the reader to savor the experience, and so he fills the stanzas with a cascade of adjectives and adverbs to describe the fullness and richness of the experience.

By the time John writes his major works, he has a very clear understanding of the entire systematization of the spiritual life. It is useful for us as we read to keep in mind the flow of the stages of the spiritual life. This awareness of the stages is useful, but John is not attached to them and neither should we be. As Edith Stein points out, "In the description of the *Spiritual Canticle* the union comes at the beginning and at the end, governing the whole. The purgation is mentioned most frequently at the transition from betrothal to marriage. The illumination accompanies the union."[28] Moreover, while the *Ascent* and the *Dark Night* focus on the darkness of purification, whereas the *Spiritual Canticle* and the *Living Flame* focus on the development of love, there are similarities and overlap, since we are always dealing with approaches to the spiritual journey. So, while one sets out in a dark night it is with anxiety and "fired with love's urgent longings" (N. stanza 1), and in all the pains of the journey what helps most of all is "the light that burned in my heart" (N. stanza 3), and after all the sufferings endured the result is that the night has united the Lover with his beloved "transforming the beloved in her Lover" (N. stanza 5).

The purgative stage of beginners (Stanzas 1-5)

The poem begins with the bride's cry of pain at being abandoned by her Beloved. She asks for help in finding him and tells the world of her fearless determination to discover where he is. The only response she gets is from creation that tells her he has passed by and left something of his own beauty in its midst. This is an extraordinary beginning of the love poem, and the depth of the bride's love is evident from the first line. So, a person begins this journey with an awareness of the meaning of life in the context of eternity (C. 1.1) and a profound longing for God, as he or she anxiously searches for union (C. 1.2). While the *Ascent* and the *Dark Night* begin with privation, the *Spiritual Canticle* begins with painful and unfulfilled longing, and then love leads the soul to want to be deprived of all that is not love of God in order to focus on love alone. "[The soul] longs for union with him through clear and essential vision. She records her longings of love and complains to him of his felt absence, especially since his love wounds her" (C. 1.2). This is a stage where the soul wishes to be deprived of everything that hinders the development of love; and this includes leaving aside previous false images of God (C. 1.3-4, 8). God inspires this enthusiasm for the search, and one soon discovers that this is a journey of transformation—a mature spiritual journey of purification and strong love. This journey starts with a deeper self-understanding and a sense of profound gratitude, as the soul receives the initial revelations of God and becomes more aware of the pervasive presence of God. This initial phase of the journey is an ongoing purification, as the soul experiences sorrow, abandonment, unfulfilled longing, and spiritual dryness. He or she learns to seek faith without understanding or satisfactions and in complete detachment. This is a time of pain and self-forgetfulness as one rejects all objects of sense, experiences the purifying effects of divine communications, and just feels sick with longing.

The development of love is only possible in a heart that is free and has overcome all attachments to creatures and controlled the snares of the soul's three great enemies—the world, the devil, and the flesh (see C. stanza 3, also "The Precautions"). The soul discovers that God is within his or her heart but hidden, and to find God one must leave aside every other interest, all former knowledge, understanding, activities of faculties of intellect, memory, and will, and satisfactions. This includes fostering an awareness of one's failures and sense of emptiness without God, cultivating a longing for God, and seeking God in faith, love, and unknowing. These are not the struggles of a seeker but those of a lover. The soul must be aware that God is not like any understandings or experiences one may have of God, and God does not act as one expects. "It is noteworthy that, however elevated God's communications and the experiences of his presence are, and however sublime a person's knowledge of him may be, these are not God essentially, nor are they comparable to him because, indeed, he is still hidden to the soul" (C. 1.3). This is where the Beloved's absences and withdrawals purify one's love (C. 1.16). A person should rejoice in the discoveries he or she makes, maintain a sense of urgency in the search, and center everything on love. Here, God is the primary actor, drawing us to divine life. God visits us and thus raises us up, and then withdraws and leaves us in painful longings of love (C. 1.22).

Since direct contact with God is not possible for human beings in this life, one can use intermediaries both to learn about God and to communicate with God. One's desires, affections, longings, and willingness to suffer let God know how much a person longs for divine union, and God welcomes these signs of love (C. 2.1). The person finds that faculties of intellect, memory, and will no longer help, and one experiences an inability in knowing God (C. 2.6). But, one learns that these intermediaries are insufficient. One must undertake a single-minded pursuit of God that has two stages: first, one must move away from self and all hindrances that are not God; second, one needs to undertake the practice of virtues and enter into assiduous contemplative prayer, and do both these with courageous perseverance (C. 3.1).

Leaving aside everything that leads one away from God, one begins to see more and more how all creation reveals the wonders of God's love, and so one carefully reads the book of creation for signs of the Beloved. "This reflection on creatures, this observing that they are things made by the hand of God, her Beloved, strongly awakens the soul to love him" (C. 4.3). One appreciates the grandeur and abundance of God's love in creation. A person can see traces of God's presence in the world and deepen his or her understanding of the mysteries of the Incarnation by which the Son clothed the world in beauty (C. 5.1). This is very different than the experience of the dark night, but it is painful, for although there is some knowledge gained in this experience, it is insufficient and brings little satisfaction, and so one's inner spirit seems torn apart, and one feels abandoned, even rejected. This is a time of early purification of love and the first steps in discovering new ways of knowing and loving.

The illuminative stage of proficients (Stanzas 6-12)

The poem began with a cry for love, but now it continues with a cry for illumination. The bride says she has had enough of mere messages, stammerings, false concepts, emptiness, miseries, and half-hearted understandings. Rather, she wants to see her Beloved face to face. "She asks him that from henceforth he no longer detain her with any other knowledge, communications, and traces of his excellence since, rather than bringing her satisfaction, these increase her longings and suffering" (C. 6.2). So, the beginnings of the spiritual life are filled with trials of bitterness, mortification, and meditation, and the soul can claim, "Among all worldly delights and sensible satisfactions and spiritual gratification and sweetness, there is certainly nothing with the power to heal me, nothing to satisfy me" (C. 6.3). However, with stanza six there is a significant change, for here the soul enters contemplation, and it is now God who draws the soul to an appreciation of the divine presence in creation (C. 6.1). In the earlier part (stanzas 1-5) the bride tries to learn how to journey to God in love, now God becomes her teacher, transforming her in contemplation. The journey in the *Spiritual Canticle* is one in which God's love gradually purifies, illumines, and transforms the soul, helping her to control appetites, learn how to love, and be transformed in union. John moves so quickly to focus on contemplation that he gives the impression that the *Spiritual Canticle* is directed to those who are already in a contemplative prayer experience (C. Prologue.3). For John the goal of contemplative life is union with God in love; this is the transformation of the soul in God. At this stage, it is illuminative, but also painful.

The world's beauty calls a person to love God, for God clothed the world in beauty to reflect the beauty of the Son, and this inspires each of us to love God. But this is painful too, for one still wants to possess God in loving union and not just see signs of God's presence (C. 6.6). However, while the bride experiences urgent longings for her Beloved, he seems distant and passive; he stirs up love, and then hides to intensify the bride's longings. When the bride tries to get close, the Beloved flees. Eventually the bride realizes that all is the work of the Beloved who draws her forward to greater love and illumines her regarding who he is and the nature of true love. While a person gains knowledge of God through irrational creatures, he or she also gains illumination through other rational creatures who reveal more about God than irrational ones do. This further knowledge causes both love and pain. This is because while one appreciates God's self-communication through creatures as a love-filled experience, it is only partial while one is restricted to bodily life, and one yearns for greater union that can only come in the next life. The illumination is painful, like a wound, a deep sore, and even death—all part of impatient love (C. 7.2-4). So, overwhelmed by God's love, one seeks deeper union and realizes only God can heal this love-sickness. At this point one longs intensely for union with God and finds no satisfaction in anything else. He or she appreciates that love seems unfulfilled, and in fact, nothing can satisfy a person except God's gift of love (C. 8.2). A person now seeks God in all things, and as he or she abandons interest in everything else, God comes close in love. John's work is a mysticism of love. There is no cure for love-sickness except in the vision of God. Such a soul feels God has called him or her to love, but is left feeling incomplete. "Such is the truly loving heart. The soul experiencing this love exclaims: 'Why do you leave it so,' that is, empty, hungry, alone, sorely wounded and sick with love, suspended in the air, and fail to carry off what you have stolen?" (C. 9.6). She feels in need of healing, nothing satisfies, everything becomes burdensome except the pursuit of love. "A characteristic of the desires of love is that all deeds and words unconformed with what the will loves will weary, tire, annoy, and displease the soul as she beholds that her desire goes unfulfilled" (C. 10.). A person longs for this intimate revelation of God's inner life of beauty, and once God gives a glimpse of divine beauty he or she would do anything to see that vision again (C. 11.2). Such a person knows the teachings of faith but longs for the substance of faith in a clear vision of God (C. 12.4-5). Then the truths are infused by God's transforming presence. One feels the intensity of longing; feels so close and yet not quite there. "The more the object of her desire comes into sight and the closer it draws, while still being denied her, so much more pain and torment does it cause" (C. 12.9). Illumination is no longer enough, the bride longs for union.

The unitive stage - part I; spiritual betrothal (Stanzas 13 - 21)

The soul has passed through the purifications of the stage of the beginners and also those of the stage of illumination. "The reason the soul suffers so intensely for God at this time is that she is drawing nearer to him; so she has greater experience within herself of the void of God, of very heavy darkness, and of spiritual fire that dries up and purges her so that thus purified she may be united with him" (C. 13.1). The will is purified and now focused on love for God alone, as the soul gives her total "yes" to God in love and in the desire for union (see F. 3.24). This total giving of self to God is a critical junction in the spiritual life and readies one for God's special gifts of grace (C. 13.1). This looks like a journey the bride is making to find her Beloved, but it is a journey made together for our efforts need the support of grace. The period of spiritual betrothal is an in-breaking of God's transforming love and includes special knowledge of God and of God's loving presence, as well as gifts and virtues for the bride. "[T]his spiritual flight denotes a high state and union of love in which, after much spiritual exercise, the soul is placed by God. This state is called spiritual betrothal with the Word, the Son of God" (C. 14-15.2). This period of betrothal prepares the soul for spiritual marriage where total transformation takes place. She feels protected from previous disturbances, but also feels the pain of the absence of the

Lover, of the wounds he causes in her heart, and of the touches of love that pierce and burn like arrows. Even the special love-filled communications cause pain, for the body cannot sustain the experience (C. 13.2, 4).

One now sees one's own gifts, longs for transformation of spiritual faculties, and yearns for the deeper union of the next stage—spiritual marriage. The bride longs to be outside of the restrictions of this present life, but the Lover, who speaks for the first time in stanza 13, urges her to remain in the struggles and growth of this life where she can give time to further purification and to learning how to love in a new way. At this time God communicates in contemplation new knowledge that leads to deeper love (C. 13.10-11). The bride, called to return to her Lover, sings of the Lover's greatness and praises, senses an end to unfulfilled love, is refreshed with special communications of God's grandeur, delight and gentleness, and peaceful love, and sees the loving presence of God in the harmony of creation (C. 14-15.2). The desire for union with God is intensified, and God passively communicates spiritual revelations.

This is both purification and enrichment, a longing for union that the soul still does not fully understand. While spiritual betrothal and spiritual marriage both belong to the unitive phase, John insisted in the *Dark Night* that the worst period of purification comes just before the stage of the perfect in spiritual marriage. It is true that he states that spiritual betrothal is a period of peace and that the painful purification is past. Yet he frequently also refers to the ongoing preparation of the times of spiritual betrothal and speaks of the painful longings of the soul and the intense pain that the soul experiences in the purification necessary for union. "During the time of the betrothal and expectation of marriage . . . the anxieties . . . are usually extreme and delicate" (F. 3.26). Several descriptions in this section are not unlike those in the *Dark Night*. This is a stage of ongoing preparation that purifies and readies the soul for the union of love. "Yet she does not say that the tranquil night is equivalent to a dark night, but rather that it is like the night that has reached the time of the rising dawn. This quietude and tranquility in God is not entirely obscure to the soul as is a dark night; but it is a tranquility and quietude in divine light, in the new knowledge of God, in which the spirit elevated to the divine light is quiet" (C. 14-15.23).

Spiritual betrothal is a high level of union in love, when God communicates knowledge and extraordinary gifts. It is also a time of peace, quiet, and enjoyment without the former pain. It is passive illumination concerning God's wisdom and love in creation, a period of vital experiences of the attributes of God, and an awareness that God is personally transforming a person. At this time he or she is possessed by the transforming power of God—an awesome experience, but without the fear and trembling of former times (C. 14-15.30). This is a knowledge that nourishes, refreshes, and deepens love—gifts of divine communication that are received passively in contemplation. It is an experience of mutuality that makes the Spiritual Canticle different from the Ascent and the Dark Night. Moreover, all this is now at the level of the spiritual faculties only. Still, all kinds of evil tendencies can disrupt the loving and delightful union. Even though a person may have sensory appetites under control, disturbances can still come, and he or she soon realizes nothing can be done without God's help (C. 16.2-3).

The seeker feels pain when the Lover is absent and when disturbances affect the focus on love. "The reason for such affliction is that since she has a singular and intense love for God in this state, his absence is a singular and intense torment for her" (C. 17.1). The Holy Spirit draws such a person out of aridity—the unfelt experience of God and the lack of consolation in prayer—while encouraging one to remember the beauty of a life of virtue (C. 17.2). Thus, the Lover communicates with the seeker and feels nourished by the life of virtue. A person now sees and appreciates his or her own gifts, yet knows union remains incomplete (C. 18.1). Suffering remains from the threat of sensory rebellions that can disturb one's peace, and the soul should pray that God protect it at this time (C. 18.3-4).

A person now asks that all divine communication be only with the spiritual faculties. This request that one's intellect, memory, and will be transformed is pleasing to God who responds by communicating special knowledge to these spiritual parts. "Since the soul desires the highest and most excellent communications from God, and is unable to receive them in the company of the sensory part, she desires God to bestow them apart from it" (C. 19.1). Now, a person longs for the next stage in the spiritual life, spiritual marriage. This development requires further purification which the Lover promises to achieve (C. 20-21.1). He gives peace and tranquility, controls the faculties, and brings to an end the negative effects of the passions (C. 20-21.16).

The unitive way—part II; spiritual marriage (Stanzas 22-40)

A. A DESCRIPTION OF TOTAL UNION IN SPIRITUAL MARRIAGE (Stanzas 22-35).

This part begins with the bride peacefully resting in the arms of her Beloved, while the Bridegroom tells the bride that his work of transformation began under the tree of the cross in redemptive grace, and continues now through his work of helping her control all negative effects of the lower appetites, helping her enter a new level of existence. Spiritual marriage is a profound transformation of the person, a revelation of special secrets, and it brings gifts of union. "This spiritual marriage is incomparably greater than the spiritual betrothal, for it is a total transformation in the Beloved, in which each surrenders the entire possession of self to the other with a certain consummation of the union of love" (C. 22.3). It includes an appreciation of God's gifts to others. It is an experience of peaceful security, mutual surrender, and equality in love. It focuses on love alone in mutual self-gift. God makes all this possible, for God is love, and here the Bridegroom's love is the point of departure (C. 22.1). God purifies former failures, and this leads to mutual gratitude and rejoicing. In spiritual marriage the beloved and the Lover surrender themselves to each other. They become one, and the beloved now participates in divine life. The Lover reveals special secrets and a deeper appreciation of the divine mysteries of the Incarnation and Redemption. He also shows how he personally redeemed each one and raised each one up to renewed life. In spiritual marriage the whole of human nature is harmoniously integrated (C. 22). This is a time to peacefully enjoy the gifts of union with one's Lover, when the beloved rejoices in the greatness and blessings of the Lover and celebrates the awareness of the many gifts and virtues that God places in the soul. There develops an equality of friendship, a mature relationship with God (C. 28.1).

This is also a time when the soul also praises and celebrates the many gifts God has bestowed on others (C. 25.1-5). A person sees, welcomes, and celebrates how God encourages others, inflames them with love, fills them with charity, and matures their love. The beloved rests secure in the transforming presence of God, for with God's grace a person has now controlled all negative disturbances of appetites, and experiences immersion in the most intimate love possible in this life. "[T]he soul relates the sovereign favor God granted by recollecting her in the intimacy of his love, which is the union with God, or transformation, through love. And she notes two effects of this union: forgetfulness or withdrawal from all worldly things, and mortification of all her appetites and gratifications" (C. 26.2).

In this contemplative union God and the beloved mutually surrender themselves to each other, and God communicates a mystical knowledge that transforms one's spiritual faculties, drawing them exclusively to divine life. "The sweet and living knowledge that she says he taught her is mystical theology, the secret knowledge of God that spiritual persons call contemplation. This knowledge is very delightful because it is a knowledge through love" (C. 27.5). Thus, God raises the seeker to the level of equality in love. In dealing with God a person dedicates all the soul's energies to love; everything is now done for love (C. 28.7). The soul appreciates that attentiveness to God and to the practice of love is the only focus of life, and leaves aside interest in everything else to focus exclusively on the love of God. In this communion each one finds his or her true purpose and destiny in life. In this mutual sharing, communion, and love, the beloved and God enjoy each other's self-gift (C. 30.2). Such a one can see how all his or her virtues, struggles, and efforts are the result of God's gifts, but somehow God values them as the beloved's efforts to become worthy of God and as a proof of love.

Then, too, a person's life of virtue is an image of God whose love has made all this possible. Now, such a person and God are bound together in strong love (C. 31.3). The soul's part was her efforts in fortitude and persevering love, and God's was the further strengthening of the soul in the fight against temptations and in fostering a life of loving fidelity. It is love alone that motivates God in dealing with the beloved, for God's nature is to love. God loves each person as a reflection of God's own love. "With God, to love the soul is to put her somehow in himself and make her his equal. Thus, he loves the soul within himself, with himself, that is, with the very love by which he loves himself. This is why the soul merits the love of God in all her works insofar as she does them in God" (C. 32.6). So, the beloved takes no credit for a life of love; it is God's gift. However, God's love is also purifying, cleansing one from all former failures. A faith-filled seeker is aware of this transformation and so takes no credit for the growth but attributes all to God. This humble acknowledgement makes one more appealing to God. This relationship of friendship and love leads both God and the person to mutual gratitude (C. 34.1). God celebrates the beloved's growth and commitment and the beloved rests in contemplative union, refreshed, protected, and blessed by God. God celebrates the beloved's peace, love, and happiness. God praises the seeker's withdrawal into solitude away from every other satisfaction. The beloved has found what he or she sought and is now alone in God. This spiritual marriage is a direct communication of divine love.

B. THE SOUL STILL LONGS FOR PERFECT UNION WITH THE BELOVED IN GLORY (Stanzas 36-40).

These last stanzas describe the state of the blessed to which the perfect now aspire. John goes on to describe the two lovers' longing for total union in glory (C. 36.3). This includes immersion in the mysteries of God, delight and gratitude, participation in the life of God, and complete harmony in union with God. Like two lovers, God and the beloved enjoy each other's company and long for ever deeper union. She rejoices in the communications of love, wants them to permeate every aspect of life, and longs to become a reflection of the beauty of God, even if this means suffering or death. In fact, a person longs for this life to end in order to enjoy the mysteries of God. Such a person and God immerse themselves in the mysteries of God, and he or she vitally experiences the attributes of God and the wonderful ways of God, and is transformed and inebriated by God's love (C. 37.5). Each one can delight in these experiences and gratefully gives glory to God. Lovers always want to love as much as they are loved, and the beloved again asks God to reveal and to teach how to love. The beloved surrenders to God in love, and God transforms and perfects this love. The soul desires "to reach the consummation of the love of God, which she had always been seeking; that is, to love God as purely and perfectly as he loves her in order to repay him by such love" (C. 38.2).

The soul is overwhelmed by this transforming vision. This contemplative vision of divine essence is an immersion in the love of God when one becomes God through participation. "Yet God accomplishes this in the soul through communication and participation. This is transformation in the three Persons in power and wisdom and love, and thus the soul is like God through this transformation" (C. 39.4). This is a foretaste of what is to come in the next life. This is human destiny—to be free of all that is not God, to be taught a new knowledge of God, and to be transformed by perfect and strong love. A person's entire being is now in harmony with the Spirit. Looking back over life a person can see former failures, appreciate the divine transformation, welcome the joy felt in one's entire being, and ask that God continue these blessings of spiritual marriage to the glorious celebration of marriage in the next life. Yet, there is no closure to the *Spiritual Canticle* for there is no end to desire.

This journey of love in the *Spiritual Canticle* offers a revolutionary vision of our approach to the stages of the spiritual journey. This is not a journey of a lonely, struggling soul in search of the unseen God. This is not a solitary pursuit of wisdom, a desire to be alone before the alone. Moreover, it does not focus on self-denial and asceticism as an exclusively negative way to God. "Where have you hidden, Beloved?" indicates from the first line that this is a journey that two lovers make together. Love is present from the beginning, as we travel in union with the Beloved. This is a rich, fulfilling, exciting journey that we undertake with warmth, excitement, and enthusiasm. Love, of course, always needs to be strong, and lovers are always ready to sacrifice in order to prove their love and deepen it. John, the doctor of divine and human love, turns so much former spirituality upside down, reminding us that in this journey God in love is accompanying us all the way, in fact, is simply taking us home.

CHAPTER SIX
KEY CONCEPTS IN THE SPIRITUAL CANTICLE (PART I--GOD)[29]

1. God, hidden and revealed

In love with a hidden God

"Where have you hidden Beloved"(C. v.1)

At the beginning of the *Spiritual Canticle* the soul already sees God as her Beloved, since she has been profoundly touched by divine love. "Tell him I love most that I am sick, I suffer, and I die without his love." However, she senses that God has already withdrawn from her and is hidden from her. "She feels . . . that God is angry and hidden because she desired to forget him so in the midst of creatures" (C. 1.1). Filled with love and fearful of losing this love, she renounces everything except the pursuit of love and profound union. She becomes aware that God will always be somewhat hidden while she remains in this life. From the first stanza the soul is not seeking sensible satisfaction but union with the divine essence which is hidden beyond human perception and knowledge. John reminds us that sometimes we make mistaken interpretations of God's presence. "Neither the sublime communication nor the sensible awareness of his nearness is a sure testimony to his gracious presence, nor are dryness and the lack of these a reflection of his absence" (C. 1.3). Even in the union of love to which this poem leads God is still hidden to the soul as long as this life lasts, for we are on pilgrimage to an awareness of the absolute otherness of God. In this journey God is primary actor, drawing us to divine life. "In the first place it should be known that if anyone is seeking God, the Beloved is seeking that person much more" (F. 3.28). God visits us and thus raises us up, then withdraws and leaves us in painful longings of love.

As the soul appreciates God's beauty and love in creation, and through others, she is inspired to love God more. But these are merely traces of God's presence and a partial understanding of God, and the soul becomes anxious for a deeper encounter beyond the constraints of the body. Likewise the Beloved gives tastes of his love, and then he seems to hide and abandon the soul who is longing for completeness and union. Partial revelations of love and of the divine presence inflame the soul and leave her aware that the Beloved is really still more hidden than revealed. Even the revelation that comes with faith still leaves the soul hungering for the real thing, not a sketch but the vision and reality of union. Partial presence feels like absence, but the soul is full of God's love and celebrates the Beloved's presence in all aspects of creation, and also in the gifts that the Beloved makes to her in the virtues of her own life.

Even in the revelations of spiritual betrothal the soul senses the hiddenness of the Beloved that still results from temptations and sensory reactions. She welcomes his communications, but they will always be somewhat hidden "until God introduces her into his divine splendors through transformation of love" (C. 13.1). So, in spite of her burning love, the Beloved tells the bride "Adapt yourself to this lower knowledge that I am communicating to you" (C. 13.8). In spiritual betrothal the Beloved reveals more of himself and his attributes, touching the bride in the very substance of her being, but even this is still "dark, for it is contemplation" (C. 14-15.16), and "Truly a hidden word" (C. 14-15. 17).

In spiritual marriage the bride hides away with her Beloved to receive the revelations in secret. In spiritual marriage each surrenders totally to the other, "two natures in one spirit and love" (C 22.3). The bride is now absorbed in love and nothing else matters; she gives herself to the Bridegroom keeping nothing back (C 27). He in turn teaches her "a sweet and living knowledge" (C 27.5). Overwhelmed, the bride is not yet satisfied and longs for deeper knowledge "deep into the thicket" (C. 36.10), where "she will know the sublime mysteries of God and human beings" (C. 37.2). Then she goes on "to the high caverns in the rock which are so well concealed" (C. 37.3), where she enjoys the knowledge, fruition, and delight of the love of God. This experience of mutual love and sharing has no name: "that which the vision of God is to the soul has no other name than 'what'" (C. 38. 6). It is inexplainable, undiscoverable, until "the day of your eternity" when the soul will be "gloriously transformed in you." For now, the soul is still in "a serene night" of contemplation, as she hears her Bridegroom calling her, and she is ready for "the glorious marriage of the Triumphant" (C. 40. 7).

Where is God hidden?

"The good contemplative must seek him with love' (C 1.6)

We find God in the revelation of the Son. "The Son is the only delight of the Father, who rests nowhere else nor is present in any other than in his beloved Son" (C. 1.5).We are all like the lover of the poem who seeks God but finds God always seems distant when we want to be close. God is hidden but we can find God as long as we understand that even when we find God it will still be in hiddenness.

In addition to the Son's revelations, the primary experience in which the Trinity is discoverable is in the depths of our own hearts. "It should be known that the Word, the Son of God, together with the Father and the Holy Spirit, is hidden by his essence and his presence in the innermost being of the soul" (C. 1.6). God is within everyone by divine essence. God is never absent from us, for in each of us there is a center which is naturally divine.

God is even hidden in the divine gifts of presence, whether by essence, grace, or spiritual affection. Even these are hidden, for "God does not reveal himself as he is, since the conditions of this life will not allow such a manifestation" (C. 11.3). God's hiding place is within us not outside us; "you yourself are his dwelling and his secret inner room and hiding place" (C. 1.7). So, we should not go searching for God elsewhere, outside of ourselves, but find God within. Nearness to God inflames greater love, reveals the Beloved, but reminds one he is more hidden than revealed (see C. 13.1). Even when the soul gets close she is told she is not ready for union and receives glimpses and intense longings, but is still told to go back (C. 13.2). No matter our own efforts, God remains hidden, and we need to appreciate the need for purification, emptiness, and receptivity.

God is sometimes hidden in the communications we receive and in the concepts we have. We must cultivate an absolute conviction of divine transcendence and let God be who God wishes to be for us. While the full revelation of God only comes in the next life, God is within our hearts but hidden. To find God we must leave aside every other interest, thus uncovering both God and our true selves. Often this means we must be aware that spiritual communications can be more our own images than God's. We must go beyond the normal objects of the faculties—intellectual knowledge, memories, and limited desires (C. 1. 12-13).

We find God still hidden in faith and we continue to seek God in faith, love, and unknowing, leaving aside all former knowledge, understanding, activities of faculties, and satisfactions (C. 1. 10-11). Often we can see better in darkness. "Only by means of faith, in divine light exceeding all understanding, does God manifest Himself to the soul" (A.2. 9.1).

God is hidden even in the touches of love given to the soul; they communicate, reveal, and wound, but they hide, too. "The soul experiencing this love exclaims: 'Why do you leave it so,' that is, empty, hungry, alone, sorely wounded and sick with love" (C. 9.6). In verse ten she goes on to insist, "Extinguish these miseries, since no one else can stamp them out." In the resulting love-sickness God both reveals and remains hidden. "The reason for this is that the love of God is the soul's health, and the soul does not have full health until love is complete" (C. 11.11).

Sometimes God is hidden because we continue to look at our own false images of God. We must remove these false gods in the dark night. "Our faith has domesticated God and effectively denied God's transcendence."[30] Clinging to our own knowledge, memories, and loves blocks a genuine revelation of God. Even religion's certainty does not lead us to truth, and a healthy insecurity and doubt concerning contemporary religion's many declarations can open us to the unseen world that can lead us to God. Our knowledge impedes God's self-revelation.

We can also see that the depressing misery of our world can hide our appreciation of God, but God's future, our hope, overwhelms and overcomes the misery and even gives meaning to what seems increasingly meaningless. Part of our contemporary misery is that we have become skilled at concealing truth, hiding from our own consciences, and blocking God's communication.

Seeking encounter with a hidden God

"All who are free tell me a thousand graceful things of you" (C. v.7)

In seeking God we need to foster an awareness of our failures and sense of emptiness without God, cultivate a longing for God, and seek God in faith, love, and unknowing which is the virtue of hope. We must be aware that God is not like any understandings or experiences we have of God, and God does not act as we expect. We should accept dryness, darkness, and emptiness, since God is often present to us in these seemingly negative experiences. We must reject all sensory satisfactions that can be found in the pursuit of spiritual values. We should rejoice in the discoveries we make, maintain a sense of urgency in the search, and center everything on love, leaving aside any affection and desire for anything other than God.

In fact, we should "let all things be as though not" (C. 1.6), leaving aside the nothingness (*nada*) of life as we focus on the all (*todo*) of God. We must go deep within ourselves in recollection and hide away with God in the depths of our own inner spirit, leaving aside interest in all else.

We do not gain more knowledge of God but discover God in faith. "Faith and love are like the blind person's guides. They will lead you along a path unknown to you, to the place where God is hidden" (C. 1.11). We can never rejoice in what we understand or experience of God but only in what we can neither understand nor experience. It is in darkness that we see who God is.

We seek God who reveals self in the dark night of contemplation, and this requires of us discipline of life, a single-minded dedication to God, priorities that focus all life in the pursuit of God, and careful correction of our faults. Then we can ready ourselves for God's illumination as we are enlightened in the dark night. Like the soul in the story we must arrive at the point of wanting no more messengers. We must be content with nothing except the revelation of God in contemplation (C. 6.1-2).

Part of our contribution is to engage in a relentless search. "Seeking my love," we must do all that is possible in a journey away from self and towards God. For this search we will need a heart that is naked, strong, and free (C. 3.5) and a clearly developed self-knowledge (C. 4.1). This search can include an appreciation of the wonders of God's love in creation (C. 4.3) insofar as they can awaken us to love God more. It will be a journey in pain and longings, in poverty of spirit, and in love (C. 1. 13-14).

2. God communicates in silence

Communication between the bride and her Lover

"This communication [is] in tranquility and solitude"
(C. 14-15. 23)

The *Spiritual Canticle* is all about the love relationship between the soul and the Bridegroom. The poem is, for the most part, a conversation between the two as they share their feelings, hopes, and love. The poem begins with the bride crying out to her unseen and absent Lover. She communicates her feelings and desires, but he gives no response. She asks a group of shepherds to pass on her message if they see him, and as she sets out to find her Lover she sees traces of his presence everywhere she goes—the whole world communicates his illuminative presence.

With stanza six the soul becomes aware that she is surrounded by silent messengers who communicate a thousand graceful things about her Beloved. He, however, seems to be teasing her, as if he is offering to communicate himself, but never does (C. 6.6). Lots of people dedicate themselves to God but their spiritual lives never pass beyond an initial commitment. The soul in the *Spiritual Canticle* wants more than indirect communication which does not have the power to heal her longing for love. However, she discovers that communication is not "out there" but within her own heart in contemplation. There, in quiet, she gets beyond the incomprehensible stammerings that pretend to communicate but convey very little.

Above all she realizes that "The Father spoke one Word, which was his Son, and this Word he always speaks in eternal silence, and in silence must it be heard by the soul" (S. 100). In union with the Son the bride finds rest, recreation, and refreshment, and she understands secrets and strange knowledge of God (C. 14-15.4). In contemplation the bride discovers a new communication of her Beloved's qualities, not just reflected in creation but essentially visible in its wonders, where God communicates and she vitally experiences the attributes of God. The Beloved communicates that he is all these qualities in himself and for her (C. 14-15). This communication is the whistling of a gentle breeze. "By 'love-stirring breezes' are understood the attributes and graces of the Beloved that by means of this union assail the soul and lovingly touch her substance" (C. 14-15.12). In her contemplation, "the soul possesses and relishes all the tranquility, rest, and quietude of the peaceful night; and she receives in God, together with this peace, a fathomless and obscure divine knowledge" (C. 14-15.22). This communication in tranquility and quietude is "the new knowledge of God, in which the spirit elevated to the divine light is in quiet" (C. 14-15.23). So, the soul experiences communication as "a whisper," the voice of a gentle wind, a revelation that is silent music and sounding solitude. "In this tranquility the intellect is aware of being elevated to the divine light in a strangely new way above all natural understandings" (C. 14-15.24).

This communication of two lovers alone is a "supper that refreshes and deepens love." It is "a symphony of love" when the soul's spiritual faculties "can receive in a most sonorous way the spiritual sound of the excellence of God" (C 14-15.26). It is a time when the visits of the Holy Spirit are like God breathing gently through the soul, communicating to her with intimate love (C. 17.8). Communication is now in silence and in secret where the soul receives "hidden wonders, alien to every mortal eye" (C. 19.3). "Hide yourself, my love, turn your face toward the mountains, and do not speak" (C. v.19).

When the bride reaches spiritual marriage, it is a communication in secret and in solitude, a time when she "has become established in the quietude of solitary love for her Bridegroom" (C. 35.1). She lives apart in solitude, quiet, simplicity, and poverty of spirit, focusing exclusively on her love for her Beloved. He delights in her solitude and silence, finds this makes her more loveable, and responds with further deeper communications of his life and love.

Transforming silence

"God teaches the soul very quietly and secretly" (C. 39.12)

God communicates in silence. Part of our understanding of the divine nature is that God communicates love internal to the Trinity and in constant gift to the world. Humanity often cannot or will not listen, but God's communication is everywhere. As an English hymn reminds us, "The whole world is aflame with God but only they who see take off their shoes." The Bridegroom praises his bride for her choice of solitude, and as their love develops she finds quiet and peaceful solitude in which she can rest alone, focusing on her love for her Beloved. So, she lived in solitude before reaching spiritual marriage in which she discovers perfect solitude, complete refreshment, and rest. In this quiet solitude, the Beloved now "guides, moves, and raises her to divine things" (C. 35.5), moving her to deeper love of God. She has learned to rest in quiet solitude, and there God communicates in silence.

We hunger for silence. Our lives are filled with noise and clutter, and in our spiritual lives, for the most part, we wander around disoriented, at best adding a new coat of paint to our spiritual lives now and again. John of the Cross presents an entire remaking of the spiritual system. He challenges us to leave aside everything from the outside and only listen to what is within. In silent attentiveness and inner recollection, we open our hearts to the transforming presence of God. In receptivity we find God in the world, in others, in divine wisdom and designs; we discover God's love for us and we become thrilled to find God teaches us how to love. The soul acknowledges that her Beloved is like "lonely wooded valleys," quiet, pleasant, delightful, refreshing, and enriching. But, it is always "in their solitude and silence they refresh and give rest" (C. 14-15.7).

John emphasizes a silent resting in the Spirit. In contemplation we hear the communications of the Holy Spirit and recognize the call to open our minds and hearts. Thus, we can listen to the unspoken communications of love for not only is the Beloved hidden, but so too is love. In silent resting we can prepare our hearts to discover both. Contemplation will be illuminative and delightful, but purgative and painful, as God gives new knowledge and strips away the old. "In contemplation God teaches the soul very quietly and secretly, without its knowing how, without the sound of words, and without the help of any bodily or spiritual faculty, in silence and quietude, in darkness to all sensory and natural things" (C. 39.12)

Transformation comes in silence. John of the Cross himself, in aloneness and abandonment, heard communications of wonder. In contemplative silence we can quiet the sensible dimensions of life and focus our spiritual vitality on the exclusive commitment to the pursuit of God's love. This means readying ourselves for divine interventions in our lives. In fruitful emptiness God guides our spiritual activity. Even in the spiritual sleep of betrothal, "the soul possesses and relishes all the tranquility, rest, and quietude of the peaceful night; and she receives in God, together with this peace, a fathomless and obscure divine knowledge" (C. 14-15.22).

Learning how to listen

"Tell me of the excellent qualities [God] has created in you"
(C. 4.7)

We must choose what to listen to. The bride comes across as a person who is very aware of life's problems. She is not dabbling in life but has a mature focus on what priorities she chooses to pursue. Communication is serious and she has a two-fold focus: rejection of all that is not God and a deliberate listening to all that leads to God. "Since seeking God demands a heart naked, strong, and free from all evils and goods that are not purely God, the soul speaks . . . of the freedom and fortitude one should possess in looking for him" (C. 3.5). So, she says she will deliberately choose what she will set her heart on, what she will tolerate, what she will pay heed to. There are so many distractions bombarding us from all sides, we need to choose what we wish to listen to and what we do not. Even in spiritual marriage the bride prefers "holy idleness" rather than the noisy accomplishments of active life and ministry (C. 29.3-4).

We must listen to our hearts. God speaks to our hearts. "I shall lead her into solitude and there speak to her heart" (Hos 2.14). The bride knows she must seek her Lover: she feels her heart is troubled, wounded, sick, unfulfilled. Her love impels her in her search, she longs for deeper union, thrills in her Lover's presence, and delights in union. While her Beloved is always drawing her to himself, she listens to her heart's longings. She lives detached from all that is not God "in profound silence of . . . senses and . . . spirit," part of a "deep and delicate listening." "God speaks to the heart in this solitude. . . in supreme peace and tranquility, while the soul listens . . . to what the Lord God speaks to it, for He speaks this peace in this solitude" (F. 3.34). Eventually, she listens only to her heart's need for her Lover, all her energy is placed at his service, she has no other interests, and everything she does is an act of love (C. v.28).

We listen to God's messengers. The *Spiritual Canticle* challenges us in the early phases of our journey to listen to God's messengers. The soul listens to her inner spirit, to the shepherds who may have seen her Beloved, to creation that reveals traces of God's presence, to others who teach a thousand graceful things of God, and to her beloved. All tell her something about God and the unceasing divine love that calls, heals, challenges, and fulfills. She listens to the revelation of God that produces a "Supper that refreshes and deepens love" (C. 14-15.28). Thus, she listens to God's messengers that give voice to divine presence in the world. "This voice is the sounding solitude the soul knows here; that is, the testimony to God that, in themselves, all things give" (C. 14-15.27).

We also listen to the challenge of John of the Cross. John is a perfect example of a person who listens to God's call to total transformation. His life evidences a relentless pursuit of union with God through early growth, reform, persecution, abandonment, and death. The fact that John attains what he does tells us that human beings are capable of this human growth and potential. Is what he achieved unusual or is it the desirable outcome for more of us? His life embodies the two great experiences of humanity—being wounded and being healed, and the *Spiritual Canticle* expresses how these two great experiences can fill the lives of us all. This book is for us; it is the life we can pursue. John writes in the broadest sense so we can each apply it personally and derive profit as best fits each of us. We must respond to John's challenge by listening carefully to the voice of God who communicates in silence deep within our hearts.

3. God's call and gift of transformation

The goal of the spiritual journey

He will bring her to . . . transformation in him through love
(C. 1.10)

Transformation takes place in spiritual marriage (C. 23-25) for which all the rest of the *Spiritual Canticle* is a preparation (asceticism (C. 1-5), illumination (C. 6-12), and spiritual betrothal (C. 13-21)). It then continues in eternity through deeper union and the revelation of the divine mysteries (C. 36-40). Transformation takes place in contemplation when we become receptive to God's activity within us, as God purifies our false desires and false gods and fills us with an inflow of divine love. We never earn or achieve transformation, but what we can do is endeavor with God's grace to conform our will to the divine. It starts with God's self-gift and we then respond by changing our lives and developing virtues. Although it is a gift, we can ready ourselves to receive this God-given transformation.

When the bride seeks the Beloved who is hidden within her heart, "he will bring her to the high perfection of union with the Son of God, her Bridegroom, and transformation in him through love" (C. 1.10). As the bride suffers the withdrawal and absence of her Beloved, the purifying pain "makes her live the life of love, transforming her in love" (C. 7.4).

Following the ascetical and illuminative phases of her journey with her initial enthusiastic longings for union, the bride enters the stage of spiritual betrothal, a preparation for when "God introduces her into his divine splendors through transformation in love" (C. 13.1). Part of this communication is the Bridegroom's gifts of virtues to adorn his bride and to prepare and season her. Later his gifts will include "transforming her into himself" (C. 17.10). Although seemingly absent, the Bridegroom is actively involved in preparing his bride for transformation. The final preparatory stage before spiritual marriage includes the Bridegroom's control of negative aspects of his bride's fantasy and imagination, anger and concupiscence, the three faculties of intellect, memory, and will, and the four passions of joy, hope, fear, and sorrow (C. 20-21.4). Once this preparation is complete, "the soul is purified, quieted, strengthened, and made stable that it may be able to receive permanently this divine union, which is the divine espousal between the soul and the Son of God" (N.2. 24.3). In this preparation through contemplation the soul is passive. This is God's work of readying us for his love. Individuals cooperate by placing no obstacles in the way and even this preparation of positive dispositions is only possible with God's help.

The goal of the spiritual journey is transformation of the bride into becoming the Bridegroom's true lover. This implies removing false loves, controlling all faculties, focusing everything on the Beloved, and becoming more and more like him in love. Transformation can be viewed in different ways as a progressive immersion in love, an ever deeper communication of divine life, a union with the Beloved in love, a mutual surrender, an identification of the bride with her Lover.

In the transformation of spiritual marriage the bride possesses her Lover and is possessed by him. This state differs from spiritual betrothal in so far as "it is a total transformation in the Beloved, in which each surrenders the entire possession of self to the other with a certain consummation of the union of love" (C. 22.3). The union is so intimate that both appear to be God. In this union, the Bridegroom transforms his bride by endowing her with gifts and virtues, giving her union, perfect love, and spiritual peace. He establishes mutuality in love, protects her from all threats, grants her habitual tranquility, and makes her equal to him in love—thus she enjoys a union of likeness with her Beloved (C. 24). The bride thus transformed in the intimacy of love enjoys these gifts in the very depths of her being. This union leads her to forgetfulness and withdrawal from all that is not conducive to this intimate love and control of all desires and pleasures in anything other than God. Now, all is enjoyed in God.

The bride's transformation in love takes place in the inner wine cellar, "the last and most intimate degree of love in which the soul can be placed in this life" (C. 26.3). It corresponds to the last stage in the development of the seven gifts of the Holy Spirit. Likewise, this transformation in the Beloved in love is also the transformation of her spiritual faculties, all now focused on the love of God. "In this transformation she drinks of God in her substance and in her spiritual faculties. With the intellect she drinks wisdom and knowledge; with the will, sweetest love; and with the memory she drinks refreshment and delight in the remembrance and feeling of glory" (C. 26.5). As God communicates the divine life they become one, so immersed in the values of God that nothing else matters, no worldly values, not even herself (C. 26.14). In her simple contemplative union she is completely purified and transformed in love (C. 26.17). "Since that act of love inflamed and transformed her into love, it annihilated her and did away with all that was not love" (C. 26.17).

As God communicates self with genuine love, they are bound to each other in mutual surrender. "And since he transforms her in himself, he makes her entirely his own and empties her of all she possesses other than him" (C. 27.6). As spiritual betrothal was a preparation for spiritual marriage, the latter becomes a preparation for the bride's total transformation into the beauty of divine wisdom when she becomes like her Beloved. This takes place in the next life when she can enter with Christ into the deepest caverns of the mysteries of God. "The soul, then, earnestly longs to enter these caverns of Christ in order to be absorbed, transformed, and wholly inebriated in the love of the wisdom of these mysteries" (C. 37.5). This she knows is not possible in this life. She wants the perfection of God's love for her and her love for God; a total communion in eternity. So, now "she desires the clear transformation of glory in which she will reach this equality" (C. 38.3). Transformation ends in consummated, perfect, and strong love. "This is transformation in the three Persons in power and wisdom and love, and thus the soul is like God through this transformation" (C. 39.4).

This transformation includes experiencing the wonders of God's life and designs, what the bride calls the indescribable "what" of joy in eternity. It will include knowing and experiencing the transforming presence of the Holy Spirit, joy in the fullness of life in God, appreciation of the harmony of creation, contemplation of the divine essence, and total transformation in love (C. 38-39). The poem ends with the bride longing for this eternal union in love; she is detached and withdrawn, evil put to flight, passions subjected, sensory part reformed, and her entire being participating in the goods of the Bridegroom to the soul. Her transformation in this life is complete and she is ready for the union of eternity.

Total commitment to the pursuit of love

"Those who truly love God must strive not to fail in this love" (C. 13.12)

We often live an illusion that the life we are living is all there is. However, anyone who reads John of the Cross must get ready for a call one never thought one would receive. John is clear that the human search for fullness of life is found in God alone; we will always be restless until we rest in the love of God. John gives us hope in his call to transformation. He tells us what can happen to humanity under the transforming power of God's love. We all struggle with our personal pain and longing to be who we are called to be—to be our best selves. The fathers of the Church defined a human being as "capax dei," capable of God. We are all called to search for union with God. In doing so we will discover God and we will also discover ourselves. This journey will always imply collapsing habits from the past, living in faith, abandoning what we previously thought worked and now know does not, and journeying to the unknown.

We can make this journey with confidence for it is not our arduous undertaking, scrambling to take a few steps forward. Rather, we are being drawn by the love of God who is always the "primary Lover." This transformation is God's work and we surrender to the divine action within us. We cannot achieve it, but we can prevent it from happening. When God wishes to send us "truth and love," all we can do is say "My heart is ready, O God, my heart is ready" (Ps. 56). We must match God's gift of selfless love with our own choice to focus exclusively on a life of love. This will be a painful journey for God does not love like we do, and our journey is learning how to love as God wills. There is only one major commitment that a human being can make, to pursue a life of love with the knowledge that nothing else matters. "You can truthfully call God Beloved when you are wholly with him, do not allow your heart attachment to anything outside of him, and thereby ordinarily center your mind on him" (C. 1.13).

Our commitment begins with the realization of our call, and we must deliberately reflect on this awesome reality. We have a personal calling to union with God in love. If we have not thought of this before, then it implies a new perception of our life, identity, and destiny. To strive for union in love is our enduring purpose in life, and this is what must motivate us in all we do. This sense of identity and enduring purpose comes from the inward journey into our heart to discover our hopes, dreams, and deepest longings. It demands the capacity to be alone in contemplative reflection, to confront our perceived limitations and our willingness to be too easily content with a half hearted calling. We are called to think about our spiritual calling in a totally different way, and this will always require humility at the greatness God has placed before us. Ultimately, spiritual growth is what God is doing in us, and so we will need to appreciate the sense of mystery of our life and surrender to this calling. Above all we must never give in to a reduced ideal of our calling. We must be totally committed to the pursuit of love.

CHAPTER SEVEN
KEY CONCEPTS IN THE
SPIRITUAL CANTICLE
(PART II—THE BRIDE)

1. Love-filled desire

The soul knows nothing save love
(C. 1.18)

"The sickness of love is not cured except by your very presence and image" (C. 11.12)

The poem of the *Spiritual Canticle* begins with a cry of intense unfulfilled longing and desire (C. v.1) and ends with the bride proclaiming that she has found what she has been seeking and desiring (C. v.38). The commentary begins with the bride who "with desires and sighs pouring from her heart, wounded with love for God" (C. 1.1) calls out to her unseen Beloved. It ends beyond spiritual marriage when the bride pleads "with the desire that he transfer her from spiritual marriage . . . to the glorious marriage of the Triumphant" (C. 40.7). The *Spiritual Canticle* is a poem of lovesick desire, wounded desire, and love-filled desire. Both poem and commentary pulsate with intense desire, draw us into this profound yearning for fulfillment, and leave us, too, inflamed with desire for God. In the first twelve verses the bridegroom never speaks, we hear only the bride's cries of anxious search; nothing really exists of importance except her desire to find her Lover.

The initial advice for the bride is quite simple: "your desired Beloved lives hidden in your heart . . . strive to be really hidden with him, and you will embrace him within you and experience him with loving affection" (C. 1.10). She soon finds it is not that simple, for the Beloved comes and goes with the swiftness of a stag, showing himself and then hiding (C. 1.15). His visits are moments of loving encounter, wounds of love, that increase the bride's desire to be with her Beloved, but he departs and she suffers pain and sorrow in his absence (C. 1.16). He leaves her suffering with love, incomplete and dying with desire for a more perfect loving union. "So extreme is this torment that love seems to be unbearably rigorous with the soul" (C. 1.18). She cries "but you were gone" and feels abandoned, suspended with no supports, and in need of the healing presence of her Lover. She appreciates the tastes of love he gives her, but rather than satisfy her desire they intensify her suffering and increase her longing (C. 1.22). "The loving soul lives in constant suffering at the absence of her Beloved, for she is already surrendered to him and hopes for the reward of that surrender: the surrender of the Beloved to her. Yet he does not do so" (C. 1.21).

The bride turns to creation and there finds traces of the beauty of her Beloved (C. 6.1), but seeing her Beloved in the beauty of the world only leads to greater desire to be in his presence; it is a sickness only union can heal. She has this same response to revelations of her Beloved through other rational beings. Eventually her desire leads her to insist: "You have communicated by means of others, as if joking with me; now may you do so truly, communicating yourself by yourself" (C 6.6). Her desire remains unsatisfied, in fact intensifies; "she is dying of love" "wounded with vehement love," and feels so restrained in this bodily life (C. 8.2). This is because she realizes that "the soul lives where she loves more than in the body she animates," and as a result she "never stops seeking remedies for her sorrow," claiming "why since you wounded this heart, don't you heal it?" (C. 9.1).

The bride's unfulfilled desire leaves her lovesick for her beloved, and she "yearns for the fulfillment and perfection of love in order to have complete refreshment therein" (C. 9.7) and good health which can only come from the healing presence of her Beloved (C. 10). When the Bridegroom sees his beloved's pain he is deeply affected by her afflictions, since they are the outcome of her loving desire. He responds by revealing deeper glimpses of divinity which do not calm her desire but even inflame it. "The more the object of her desire comes into sight and the closer it draws, while still being denied her, so much more pain and torment does it cause" (C. 12.9).

The bride's desire matures in interaction with her Beloved. Her desire for perfect union and transformation intensifies as she approaches spiritual marriage and the finishing stages of purification (C. 20-21.3). Desire is not only for greater union but also to be rid of temptations and disturbances. In spiritual marriage her desires are met. "She finds in this state a much greater abundance and fullness of God, a more secure and stable peace, and an incomparably more perfect delight than in spiritual betrothal" (C. 22.5). Yet desire remains the guiding power in her life. At the end of her journey to encounter her Lover she is still dying with the desire to penetrate the incomprehensibility of divine judgments (C. 36.11) and desires the suffering that brings her to the divine wisdom and loving union for which she always longed. Along the way of her search her desire has grown into the realization that what she really wants is "to love the Bridegroom as perfectly as he loves her" (C. 38.2), and she longs for him to teach her "to love purely, freely, and disinterestedly as he loves us" (C. 38.4).

The nature of desire

"Stricken by love . . . I lost myself and was found" (C. v 29)

Desire is not easily satisfied. When John speaks of desire he is describing an attitude of the whole person, an existential yearning or longing to be who we are called to be, who we need to be in order to find peace and fulfillment in life. When John speaks of desire he is describing what is at the core of our humanity. The desire he describes is the cry of humanity for fulfillment in the union of love.

Desire's original focus is on "your Beloved whom you desire and seek" (C. 1.8). Having fallen in love the desire is now for a deeper experience of something that has already happened. Since the soul has already been swept off her feet by her Lover her journey is always painful at her loss, but the pain is tolerable because of her confidence in her Lover's fidelity. As the search develops, "It seems to the soul that its bodily and spiritual substance is drying up with thirst for this living spring of God." She feels her desire can only end when "she could plunge into the unfathomable spring of love" (C. 12.9). Being with one's Lover is the only thing that matters— to lose oneself for the Beloved and to lose interest in all creatures. "And this is to love herself purposely, which is to desire to be found" (C. 29.10).

We then respond to desire within our own hearts. The desire John presents is the human heart seeking meaning and fulfillment and finding them in love. It is no use seeking fulfillment in the accumulation of desires outside ourselves. "Do not go in pursuit of him outside yourself. You will only become distracted and wearied thereby, and you shall not find him, or enjoy him more securely, or sooner, or more intimately than by seeking him within you" (C. 1.8). So, desire is fulfilled in the interior recollection of our own hearts, for our Lover resides within. "Desire him there, adore him there" (C. 1.8) for he whom your soul loves is within you.

These visits of love intensify desire. While our desire seems at times to burn us up, we also quickly see it is God who desires the love relationship and he is the first Lover. So, God visits the soul frequently during her desire-filled search for her Lover. However, she experiences these visits of love with joy and excitement, but also with pain. In fact, her desire is not fulfilled nor even calmed by these visits. Rather, she experiences them as wounds in her heart—wounds of love that cause a longing for total love. So, these visits of love are not simply refreshing experiences offered by her Lover. "He bestows these to wound more than heal and afflict more than satisfy, since they serve to quicken knowledge and increase appetite (consequently the sorrow and longing) to see God" (C. 1.19)

The soul tries every means to satisfy desire. Desire by itself is not enough, we must do something about it, we must do all we can to satisfy it. "Since the desire in which she seeks him is authentic and her love intense, she does not want to leave any possible means untried. The soul that truly loves God is not slothful in doing all she can to find the Son of God, her Beloved" (C. 3.1). Among the primary means are the uprooting of false loves, the practice of virtues, and the spiritual exercise of active and contemplative life. Everything that is not focused on desire for God is a distraction. We must be careful for we become our desires and for the most of us our desires are too small. Fortunately, the night is the death of all false desires, all false gods. The search is filled with "a thousand displeasures and annoyances" (C. 10.3) that can easily distract the search and this demands constant effort. Desiring to reach God in spiritual marriage, "it is necessary for her to attain an adequate degree of purity, fortitude, and love" (C. 20-21.2).

Desire is for greater love and union, from early stages of love and excitement in pursuing her Lover, through periods of pain and loss at his absence, and on to spiritual betrothal and marriage. "The loving soul, however great her conformity to the Beloved, cannot cease longing for the wages of her love . . . the wages of love are nothing else . . . than more love, until perfect love is reached" (C. 9.7). The soul is filled with impatient love that allows no rest, no delays in the ongoing pursuit of greater love. Desire for deeper love and union is what propels and motivates the soul in her ceaseless pursuit of her Lover. This intense desire focuses on seeking the beauty and essence of God. "Reveal your presence, and may the vision of your beauty be my death" (C. 11. 1-2).

Nurturing desire

"He whom my soul loves is within me" (C. 1.9)

We should always identify the desires of our lives. Desire is the human response to what will make us complete. It shows us the direction of a pilgrimage we undertake to find fulfillment, to find ourselves, to find the love for which we were created. This yearning within us cries out, "show me what my soul has been seeking" (C. v.38). Once we identify the desire of life, it becomes the motivating force for all we do.

As we pursue desire with single-minded dedication, *we must first of all purify our desires.* Our desires define us. We seek something or someone so intensely it takes the place of God. When we abandon all false desires, false gods, we lose ourselves and find our true selves (C. v.29). We must undertake this journey with excitement and enthusiasm and let nothing digress or distract us. "A characteristic of the desires of love is that all deeds and words unconformed with what the will loves will weary, tire, annoy, and displease the soul as she beholds her desire goes unfulfilled" (C. 10.5). Some grow weary in this journey and many abandon the effort. We must follow our desire unceasingly, with deliberate and intense longing.

Let your heart be drawn by God. Desire is placed in our hearts by God who longs to satisfy our desire more than we do. God is the prime Lover who has placed this yearning within us. He calls us personally, fills the world with reminders of his love, illumines us, and transforms us in contemplation.

Appreciate the signposts that direct to desire. We are immersed in God's love. All around us are signs that help us clarify and intensify our desire. We see traces of the love we seek in creation, in God's works, wonders, and decrees, in other human beings and in the spiritual world—all reminding us of the intensity of desire for the source of all this love. These signs of our Lover's desire nurture our hearts, constantly communicate to us, and let us know where true love lies. Even our own initial desires, and more so as they grow, act as messengers showing us both what our hearts desire and also what the Beloved longs for. This illumination from creatures produces immense appreciation and love of God and a resulting intense impatient love.

Only a life of love satisfies desire. John makes us aware of deep desires that we have, a hunger that cannot be satisfied except we make this journey of love. Following our desire means learning how to love until we find "the perfection of love . . . [and] complete refreshment therein" (C. 9.7). As we follow our desire God teaches us to love with the very strength with which God loves us (C. 38.4).

2. Surrender to strong love

God values strong love (C. 31.5)

"This love is the end for which we were created" (C. 29.3)

From the beginning of both poem and commentary, the bride's love is very strong, she is determined in her approach to her Beloved, and she is clearly willing to do and endure whatever it takes to find union in his love. She knows her obligations, appreciates the dynamics of salvation history, is well aware of her indebtedness to God, and saddened by the evil and harm she sees in the world (C. 1.1). During the experiences of this journey her love will mature as she learns to let go of false loves and to discover new ways of loving (C. 1.2). However, from the first step she does everything under the powerful motivation of strong love (C. 1.2) and with readiness to persevere in her love and sacrifice everything else to gain or receive it (C. 1.13). To her initial determined self-gift and self-forgetfulness she adds acceptance of the burning pain that her Lover's treatment causes. "She loves him more than all things when nothing intimidates her in doing and suffering for love of him whatever is for his service" (C 2.5).

Soon after her relationship begins and she thinks loving union is close at hand, she discovers that "love seems unbearably rigorous with the soul" (C 1.18) and that true love includes purification of all appetites, focus of intellect, will, and memory, mortification and penance, spiritual exercises, and the reception of God's gifts in contemplation. Intense love such as this requires freedom and fortitude, "Since seeking God demands a heart naked, strong, and free from all evils and goods that are not purely God" (C. 3.5). The soul finds some solace is feeling filled with love on seeing traces of her Beloved in the beauty of the world and cries out "If up to this time I could be content with [indirect knowledge], because I did not have much knowledge or love of you, now the intensity of my love cannot be satisfied with these messages; therefore: 'Now wholly surrender yourself!'" (C. 6.6).

The soul continues to surrender herself to her Beloved, to love him in every way she can, and to continue to prepare herself to love more purely and intensely. She pleads for healing which can only come from love, and she continues her fight against temptations and disturbances caused by the world, the devil, and the flesh. In this period the soul needs steadfastness and courage, bravery against all fears, and strength to persevere. When the soul is in the midst of the darkness and voids of her struggles, the Bridegroom sends her signs of his love, "divine rays with such strong love and glory" (C. 13.1). Thus, he repays her surrender and strong love with his strong love, and he continues to do this, adapting his visits of intense love to the intensity of her love (C. 13.2). At this time of intense burning love, the Holy Spirit comes to her in contemplation as a refreshing breeze that both cools and inflames her love. "As a breeze cools and refreshes a person worn out by the heat, so this breeze of love refreshes and renews the one burning with the fire of love" (C. 13.12).

Spiritual betrothal is a time of deeper love and mutual surrender; the two lovers feel each other's pain, share ever deeper communications, appreciate each other's longings, show mutual gratitude for graces and gifts, and yearn for union. The bride develops "a singular and intense love for God," and "his absence is a singular and intense torment for her" (C. 17.1). In this growth of love and self-surrender "a singular fortitude and a very sublime love are also needed for so strong and intimate an embrace from God" (C. 20-21.1). Even before spiritual marriage she gives her love and surrender to her Bridegroom (C. 22.5).

Spiritual marriage is the time of mutual strong love and surrender. God shows the soul genuine love, the tenderness and truth of love, supreme and generous love. The bride is "dissolved in love" and "she makes a complete surrender of herself." "[T]his mutual surrender of God and the soul is made in this union" (C. 27.2). "In this stanza the bride tells of the mutual surrender made in this spirit of espousal between the soul and God . . . joined by the communication he made of himself to her, . . . and by the complete surrender she made of herself to him, keeping nothing back for herself" (C. 27.3). The bride's total surrender is caused by God, it is a gift to the bride of the necessary purity, perfection, and self dedication needed for total surrender (C. 27.6). Her surrender in loving union includes the surrender of her soul and its faculties so that they focus only on love of God and what pleases God. She surrenders to a consuming love and her every expression becomes an act of love. The bride puts it this way: "This is like saying that now all this work is directed to the practice of love of God, that is: All the ability of my soul and body . . . move in love and because of love. Everything I do I do with love, and everything I suffer I suffer with the delight of love" (C. 28.8).

The Bridegroom and bride now enjoy mutuality in love and in self-surrender, enjoying each other's love. "God not only values this love of hers because he sees that it is alone, but also cherishes it because he sees that it is strong. . . . [T]his is why he loved her so much; he saw that her love was strong . . . alone and without other loves" (C. 31.5). Transformed in love, her love is now God's love in her. She is united to God's strong love for her, and "her love for him is as strong and perfect as his love for her" (C. 38.3).

Romantic love

"The lover does not possess her heart but has given it to the Beloved" (C. 9.2)

John proclaims divine love with great tenderness that uses human love as its point of departure. In the *Spiritual Canticle* John of the Cross describes the growing relationship of two lovers. The poem is full of intimacy, passion, intensity, sensualness, and a longing for union—all of which take hold of the reader. It is not only that in reading it we can think of our intimate relationship to God but we can also think of our passionate desire and intimate longing for our own lover. We already saw one author summarize what several have implied, "This monk can give lessons to lovers."[31] There is a profound affective sensuous dimension to John's poetry. He could not write like he does without feeling as we do when we read it. Clearly, in spite of his emphasis on purification, John does not propose the destruction of sense but the total unification of affectivity towards God. He also indicates that we rediscover sense refined at the end of purification. Was John totally detached from the sensory pleasure of his work? When we witness such clumsy and selfish approaches to love today, it is refreshing to read the sensitive, delicate, considerate, and, yes, sensual and passionate approaches he describes and suggests.

There is no explicit religious language in the poem. It is a poem about lovers. In his commentary he gives profound religious explanations but intertwined are comments about the approaches of lovers to each other. Here is a short selection of his many comments.

"Lovers are said to have their hearts stolen or seized by the object of their love" (C. 9.5).

"[S]he affectionately calls him here the light of her eyes, just as a lover would call her loved one the light of her eyes in order to show her affection" (C. 10.8).

"Supper affords lovers refreshment, satisfaction, and love" (C. 14-15.28).

"[G]irls attract lovers to themselves by their affection and grace" (C. 18.4).

"Anyone truly in love will let all other things go in order to come closer to the loved one" (C. 29.10).

"New lovers are comparable to new wine. . . .These new lovers find their strength in the savor of love." (C. 25.10).

"Now then, the old lovers . . . are like old wine . . . these lovers taste the sweetness of the wine of love" (C. 25.11).

"Strange it is, this property of lovers, that they like to enjoy each other's companionship alone" (C.36.1)

"The reason they desire to commune with each other alone is that love is a union between two alone" (C. 36.1).

"For lovers cannot be satisfied without feeling that they love as much as they are loved" (C. 38.3).

The first thing that John teaches lovers is to value love alone above all else. This will imply risk, but God's love of us is such that God is willing to take a risk with us. Once a commitment is made then one's capacity for love depends on the exclusive and integrated focus of every aspect of one's life. Love implies total self-surrender to one's lover; it is never stationary but always in movement—a long journey in which love matures gradually. Together they find "mutual refreshment and renewal in love" (C. 13.2).

John knows the importance between lovers of keeping a diligent watch over one's heart. At the beginning of the poem the bride sees in herself a lot of conscious and unconscious resistance to God's love and illumination and needs the purification of false loves and attachments (C. 1.1). In searching for her beloved she refuses to digress (C. 3.5), nor be tempted by enemies of her single-hearted pursuit (C. 3.6-7). As she gets closer to her Beloved she still keeps in check "many various kinds of images . . . brought to the memory and phantasy and many appetites and inclinations . . . stirred up in the sensory part" (C. 16.4). She longs for her heart to be carefully centered on her Beloved and to resist the negative drying up of interest that comes with "the foxes" (sensory movements) (C. v.16), the "deadening north wind" (dryness) (C. v.17), or the "girls of Judea" (lower affections) (C. v. 18). Once she enters spiritual marriage Aminadab (the devil) no longer appears, the siege is stopped (appetites and passions), and the cavalry descends (all bodily senses are controlled) (C. v. 40). A diligent watch over one's heart helps the bride to maintain an exclusive focus on her Lover. "Deny your desires and you will find what your heart longs for" (S. 15).

Lovers always find it is difficult to be away from each other and also they often feel unworthy of each other when they are together. They savor the pain of both absence and presence. "Beholding that the bride is wounded with love for him, because of her moan he also is wounded with love for her. Among lovers, the wound of one is a wound for both" (C. 13.9). Prior to spiritual betrothal the "wounds" of love of the bride are mentioned twenty-five times. These experiences of pain at the Lover's absence feel like a fire of love, enflamed within her (C. 1.17), and she tells him she is dying without him, wants nothing but him alone, feels unhealthy and incomplete without him, feels he has stolen her heart and nothing else matters anymore. Through these purifying wounds her love becomes impatient, burning, ardent, intense, and vehement. This purification becomes a progressive surrender to love. As the bride in the Song of Songs (8:6-7), the bride here indicates that nothing can quench love, neither floods drown it; she clearly wants her Lover as a seal upon her soul, for love is as strong as death.

Lovers want total self-gift from each other; partial gift is not what lovers want to give nor want to receive. They seek from each other what the psalms call "steadfast love," that is "precious," and "better than life" (Pss 36, 63, 89). In the *Spiritual Canticle* the bride tells her Lover do not hide, do not send me any more messengers, wholly surrender yourself, how can I endure not living where you live. She insists – carry me off, cure my love-sickness, extinguish my pain from your absence, reveal your presence. She sees her Lover's gifts and signs of his presence everywhere—everything reminds her of him and speaks of his love.

She rests in his delight, finds her bed is in flower, enters the inner wine cellar of love, loses interest in all else, gives herself totally to him, and now she wounds him with her love. She has found her longed-for mate, finds love in solitude with him, and discovers her Lover in new ways never before imagined.

3. Immersion in God's beauty

Sharing the beauty of God

"Let us go forth to behold ourselves in your beauty" (C. v. 36)

Every page of the *Spiritual Canticle* celebrates beauty. The bride rejoices in all aspects of creation, the mountains, lonely wooded valleys, strange islands, and so on. John shares with the bride the prayer of St. Francis, "My God and all things," for she feels that all things are God (C. 14-15.5). John also sees God's beauty in people, "Oh, then, soul, most beautiful of all creatures" (C. 1.7). For John, sin is the absence of beauty, and he looks at it with sadness rather than being judgmental. The spiritual journey is God's progressive revelation of divine life to the bride, and she immerses herself more and more in the knowledge of her Lover. John shares his knowledge of this journey with his readers, fully aware that "not even they who receive these communications" are able to "describe. . . the understanding [God] gives to loving souls in whom he dwells" (C. Prologue.1). He agrees with theologians and philosophers that we know God primarily through the divine attributes, and he lists them in both the *Ascent* and the *Living Flame* (A. 2. 26.3, F. 3.2). "God in his unique and simple being is all the powers and grandeurs of his attributes. He is almighty, wise, and good; and he is merciful, just, powerful and loving, etc.; and he is the other infinite attributes and powers of which we have no knowledge" (F. 3.2). In the journey the bride not only knows these qualities of God but experiences them vitally, penetrating their meaning for her life. Mystics rarely add to the traditional list of divine attributes, but John singles out one attribute that was very special to him—divine beauty. He uses this word to describe God, always using the noun form *hermosura* (beauty) rather than the adjective *hermoso* (beautiful). This unusual description is not used analogically from the beauty of nature, but rather is clearly intended to refer to the inner being of God. Thus, the bride asks God "to show her his beauty, his divine essence" (C. 11.2). So, for John beauty is a divine attribute equivalent to the divine essence.

In two passages John seems swept off his feet when he thinks of God's beauty. In one of them he uses the word "beauty" twenty-four times in a single paragraph (C. 36.5) and in the other six times in four lines (C. 11.10). Mother Francisca de la Madre de Dios testified that on one of his visits to Beas, sometime in 1582-1584, John was carried away by the thought of the beauty of God and wrote five additional stanzas of the *Spiritual Canticle* on the beauty of God (36-40). People who study the mystics refer to the constant repetition of a concept as "mystical obsession." In this case, John seems so overwhelmed by the thought of God's beauty that it could be part of his own original experience of God.

Even in the early illuminative phase of contemplation the bride seeks the presence of God and identifies it as beauty, longing "to see him in his divine being and beauty." In response to her longings, "God communicates to her some semi-clear glimpses of his divine beauty" (C. 11.4). This intensifies her longing for more intimate presence, but with this comes the awareness that such a vision is not possible, for human nature cannot endure such a revelation in this life. Thus, the bride cries "may the vision of your beauty be my death" (C. 11.16); she is willing to die to have the vision of God's beauty. In the meantime she affirms her faith "which contains and hides the image and the beauty of her Beloved" (C. 12.1), just a sketch of the reality. She experiences God's beauty all around her (C. 24.6) and longs to see herself in the beauty of God (C. 37.1). Her lovesickness climaxes in the ecstatic cry for union in eternity: "Let us rejoice, Beloved, and let us go forth to behold ourselves in your beauty" (C. v.36).

"This means: Let us so act that by means of this loving activity we may attain to the vision of ourselves in your beauty in eternal life. That is: That I be so transformed in your beauty that we be alike in beauty, and both behold ourselves in your beauty, possessing then your very beauty; this, in such a way that each looking at the other may see in the other their own beauty, since both are your beauty alone, I being absorbed in your beauty; hence, I shall see you in your beauty, and you will see me in your beauty, and I shall see myself in you in your beauty, and you will see yourself in me in your beauty; that I may resemble you in your beauty, and you resemble me in your beauty, and my beauty be your beauty and your beauty my beauty; wherefore I shall be you in your beauty, and you will be me in your beauty, because your very beauty will be my beauty; and thus we shall behold each other in your beauty" (C. 36.5).

Appreciation of the world

"[W]ith his image alone, [he] clothed them in beauty" (C. v.5)

John loved the beauty of the world, enjoyed time alone in the cave in Segovia, loved to take his friars for walks at El Calvario, and saw beauty all around him in Granada. He was a man of sacrifice and detachment who also appreciated the world around him. "If you purify your soul of attachments and desires, you will understand things spiritually. If you deny your appetite for them, you will enjoy their truth, understanding what is certain in them" (S. 49). When you view the world through a different lens, everything changes. For John love made him see everything in a new way, in a real way. In the early part of the journey creatures are means but insufficient to lead to God, and one must detach oneself from everything. However, in the ascetical phase of the journey "the consideration of creatures is first in order after the exercise of self-knowledge" (C. 4.1) for it helps us appreciate the greatness of God's love and generosity in creation, and this awakens our love for God (C. 4.1,3). "Only the hand of God, her Beloved, was able to create this diversity and grandeur" (C. 4.3). But the bride feels overwhelmed with love for her Beloved as she sees traces of his presence in creatures, and she becomes "anxious to see the invisible beauty that caused this visible beauty" (C. 6.1).

Later, in God all is transformed and one can return to the beauty of everything in God, for all the world now speaks of the presence of the Beloved. John includes the whole cosmos in his loving appreciation: "woods" are the basic elements of the universe, "thickets" refer to the teaming of animals, "green meadows" are the stars and planets, and "flowers" are angels and saintly souls (C. v.4). One of the results of spiritual betrothal is that "In that nocturnal tranquility and silence and in the knowledge of the divine light the soul becomes aware of Wisdom's wonderful harmony and sequence in the variety of her creatures and works" (C. 14-15.25). It is interesting that John changes tense from "created" to "carry on," from past tense to present, for God is still working now, manifesting his glory through creation all around us (C. 4.3).

John is always showing us how to discover openings into the inner world of God's love. One author suggests that the *Spiritual Canticle* represents "a reordering of the cosmos, a world made new," and as we read the *Spiritual Canticle* "we begin to see that world differently and sense something of its beauty and wonder."[32] Creation is now an efficacious sacrament of God's love. Creation is beautiful because God gazed on it, and when we look at the world in contemplation we encounter the loving actions of God. In the early part of the book, John presents creation as a reflection of God's loving presence, where the woods and thickets are planted by the hand of the Beloved. Later, creation is no longer only a reflection but now there is identification: "My Beloved, the mountains." Moreover, even though living in the times of the Inquisition, John does not seem willing to correct this, for now he truly is in love with the mountains, the lonely wooded valleys, and so on. For John this is due to the fact that the Son identified with the world in the Incarnation (C. 5.4, 37.1).

As we look on the world today, we see God's wisdom and judgment in the wonders of all around us. "God created all things with remarkable ease and brevity, and in them he left some trace of who he is" (C. 5.1). The world gives us illumination concerning God. Sometimes God's creation is so awesome that there is often an "I-don't-know-what" behind the communication (C. 8.1). "[I]n the living contemplation and knowledge of creatures the soul sees such fullness of graces, powers, and beauty with which God has endowed them that seemingly all are arranged in wonderful beauty and natural virtue" (C. 6.1). The world calls us to God and urges us to appreciate the hidden presence of love that surrounds us.

CHAPTER EIGHT
THE IMAGE OF GOD IN
THE SPIRITUAL CANTICLE

In the "Romances" the Father wants to show the Son how deeply he loves him, and so extends his love by giving the Son a bride. In returning his love for his Father, the Son says he will love his bride as a way of showing his love for the Father. The *Spiritual Canticle* describes this loving exchange. It is primarily the work of God, even though it is wrought by the Son through the power of the Holy Spirit. "Three Persons, and one Beloved among all three. One love in them all makes of them one Lover and the Lover is the Beloved in whom each one lives." (Romance 1). John does not think about God in distinctions. At one time the Son is the Beloved and at other times God. John's is a mystical vision of God's transforming love, and while we look at the activities of each Person, we need to keep in mind John's free movement from one to the other as part of his unified vision, which is doctrinally sound and spiritually dynamic.

God—the principal lover (C. 31.2)

The Spiritual Canticle is a book about the love of God. John composed this work "with a certain burning love of God" and he believes that the soul who reads it will be informed and moved by "the wisdom and charity of God." He points out that not all readers will understand everything, but if moved by love we can love God without understanding him (C. Prologue). As we read let us keep in mind that our communications and experiences are never essentially God, no matter how exceptional we think them to be. In fact, we have no assurance of ever being in the grace of God or not (C. 1.4). The assurance we do have is that God is never absent from the soul, and if the soul enters into hiddenness God will bring her to union and transformation with the Son (C. 1.10). So, we can undertake this journey with confidence.

God challenges us to unlearn old ways of loving. Since God is hidden, this journey to God is one of negation of our former faith, love, understanding, and satisfactions (C. 1.12). God values our love, he is our Beloved, and a soul should only call him "Beloved" if she truly loves him, for "Nothing is obtained from God except by love" (C. 1.13). It is interesting that here the Beloved is clearly God, whereas elsewhere the Beloved refers to Christ. In this journey to encounter God the soul realizes that nothing satisfies except God, and God is possessed through poverty of spirit (C. 1.14). In this journey, God visits the soul, wounds it, raises it up, bestows secret knowledge, and enflames the soul with love (C. 1.17). Also God transforms the soul's appetites and affections, leaving her with a painful longing to see God and with a profound sense of absence that deepens the longing to see God (C. 1.19). God alone can heal these wounds of love, but at first attracts the soul through intermediaries (C. 2.1). God listens to the yearnings of the soul and will hear them at the appropriate time; God appreciates the soul's efforts and urges her to continually seek to find. At the same time, God allows temptations to those he wants to strengthen and raise up (C. 3.5), and the soul soon knows that only God can overcome the evils she must confront. This is a time of purification and of abandoning old ways of loving.

In contemplation God illumines and teaches love. The soul who seeks knowledge of God must first have self-knowledge and knowledge of creation. She appreciates that the Creator manifests self in creation and knows that only the hand of God, her Beloved, could create such diversity and she can see that God has left a trace of self in creation (C. 5. 1). Part of this appreciation is to see that God united the divinity with creation in the Incarnation and the mysteries of faith, and the Son raised up creation by taking human nature himself (C. 5.4). Thus, through contemplation God illumines the whole world, and the lover finds the beauty of the Beloved in creation (C. 6.1). In this phase of illumination the soul sees that we have life and being in God (C. 8.3), and we must strive for deeper union with God. The gift of perfect love will be the reward for all one's efforts (C. 9.7). In fact, God is always ready to satisfy needs when the soul has no interest in anything but God (C. 10.6). There is pain in this journey, but the loving Bridegroom cannot long watch the soul suffering, after all it was God who placed and encouraged these painful longings in her soul. "In this spiritual sense of his presence, he revealed some deep glimpses of his divinity and beauty by which he greatly increased her fervor and desire to see him" (C. 11.1). God is present by essence, by grace, and by affection although still hidden, and it is through the hiddenness of faith that one attains spiritual espousal with God, but at this early stage God communicates self to us only through this sketch of faith. "Over this sketch of faith the sketch of love is drawn in the will of the lover. When there is union of love, the image of the Beloved is so sketched in the will, and drawn so intimately and vividly, that it is true to say that the Beloved lives in the lover and the lover in the Beloved" (C. 12.7). Thus, God dwells in the soul like a sketch on her soul, for total transformation comes only in the next life (C. 12.8).

God transforms the soul in love. The transition to spiritual betrothal is painful, for when God does not communicate to the soul there is a painful void. When the soul is in this darkness, God grants favors to her in the measure of her darkness. Gradually, God introduces the soul into divine splendors through transformation in love. "The reason the soul suffers so intensely for God at this time is that she is drawing nearer to him; so she has greater experience within herself of the void of God, of very heavy darkness, and of spiritual fire that dries up and purges her so that thus purified she may be united to him" (C. 13.1). At this time, amidst her trials, the Beloved visits the soul with strong love (C. 13.2) and does so in accord with the intensity of her yearnings. As the bride yearns for the Beloved, he communicates something of the divine self, and the bride is taken outside of herself in contemplation. Unable to cope with this communication, the bride asks him to withdraw her limitations so she can be in greater union, but the Bridegroom insists that this soul, wounded with his love, must return to this world for greater purification, for human nature cannot yet receive communications like these (C. 13.3, 8). Now the Bridegroom himself feels like a wounded stag, running around in pain, as he sees and feels the pain of his bride (C. 13.9).

These communications come in contemplation; they are extraordinary but still hidden as they always will be in this life. "However sublime may be the knowledge God gives the soul in this life, it is but like a glimpse of him from a great distance" (C. 13.10). The Bridegroom comes to the soul not in the knowledge but in the love caused by this knowledge. As love is the union of the Father and the Son, so this love is the union of the soul with the Son. Even the Bridegroom gains refreshment from the bride's love, for love enkindles love (C. 13.12). In this state of spiritual communication, spiritual betrothal, God grants love to the soul according to her desire and love, and he communicates and enriches the soul in peace. "[T]his spiritual flight denotes a high state and union of love in which, after much spiritual exercise, the soul is placed by God. This state is called spiritual betrothal with the Word, the Son of God" (C. 14-15.2). This union with God gives rest, knowledge, peace, strength, gratification, wisdom, appreciation of harmony in creation. It brings the soul an experience of the attributes of God, removes evils from the soul, and fills her with blessings. These blessings are not distinct from the Bridegroom, for he is all the above for the soul; "in this possession the soul feels that God is all things for her" (C. 14-15.5).

At this time, the Beloved's visits throw light on the bride's virtues (C. 16.1); she blossoms in union with the Bridegroom, and values his continual help (C. 16.8). However, when he absents himself, the bride feels intense pain (C. 17.1), and when he communicates with her, the supernatural brings pain because of the limitations of human nature. "Since I go to you through a spiritual knowledge strange and foreign to the senses, let your communication be so interior and sublime as to be foreign to all of them" (C. 19.7). This intimate embrace of God in spiritual marriage requires rigorous purification. This union is a "powerful and intimate bond effected between God and her (the soul)" (C. 20-21.1).

God grants a mutual celebration of transforming love. God calls the bride to spiritual marriage after some time in the mutual love of betrothal, and thus again draws good from evil by the cross. Spiritual marriage between the Son and the soul is now effected (C. 22.3), and the Beloved brings about total transformation and consummation in union as the two natures become one in spirit and love. The bride is now united with God in transformation, is liberated from all disturbances, and receives the "kiss" of union with God (C. 24.5). She offers her virtues as a sign of God's love. "Thus all these virtues are present in her as though hung with the love of God, as in a subject in which they are well preserved. And they are as though bathed in love because each one of them is ever enkindling her love of God, and in all things and in all works they move her with love to love God more" (C. 24.7). At this time God leaves a trace of the divine self in the soul that enables her to run lightly in the pursuit of God; thus God inflames her with a touch of love and enkindles her will in the love of God (C. 25.4). God clothes the soul, bathing her in divinity; God communicates self in this final step of love and the experience is beyond words (C. 26.4). This communication transforms the faculties of intellect, memory, and will by means of the three theological virtues of faith, hope, and charity (C. 26.5). God's presence in the soul enables her to value supernatural knowledge and to place no value on anything else. However, in this act of love and unknowing even natural knowledge is joined to the wisdom of God (C. 26.16). Thus, God communicates the divine self to the soul in genuine love, and causes in the soul the purity and perfection necessary for total surrender (C. 27.6). God values nothing but love and is pleased only with the soul's love (C. 28.1). While God is always "the principal lover," God looks at the bride's strong love and values it (C. 31.5). God's gaze cleanses, endows with grace, and illumines the soul; God willingly forgets former sins even though the bride would do well not to do so.

God's love now leads to equality. "With God, to love the soul is to put her somehow in himself and make her his equal. Thus he loves the soul within himself, with himself, that is, with the very love by which he loves himself. This is why the soul merits the love of God in all her works in so far as she does them in God" (C. 32.6). God deeply appreciates the transformation in love wrought in the bride (C. 33.9), a transformation of intellect, will, and memory. Now God is the soul's guide (C. 35.1), showing the soul how to love. "Besides teaching her to love purely, freely, and disinterestedly, as he loves us, God makes her love him with the very strength with which he loves her" (C. 38.4). Now, there is perfect union between the soul and God, and God leads her deep into the thicket of the revelation of the mysteries of God (C. 37.2).

The Trinity—the beginning and end of love and union

John refers to the Trinity once at the beginning of the *Spiritual Canticle* and then afterwards only in part four which deals with the bride's longing for total union in eternity. When the bride asks where the Beloved is hidden, John writes: "It should be known that the Word, the Son of God, together with the Father and the Holy Spirit, is hidden by his essence and his presence in the innermost being of the soul" (C. 1.6). That is where the lover should seek him and at the end of all her efforts, as she yearns for eternal union, John then writes: "There would not be a true and total transformation if the soul were not transformed in the three Persons of the Most Holy Trinity in an open and manifest degree" (C. 39.3). In this spiritual marriage, "God favors her by union with the Most Blessed Trinity, in which she becomes deiform and God through participation" (C. 39.4). At this time the soul understands, knows, and loves "in the Trinity, together with it, as does the Trinity itself! . . . This is transformation in the three Persons in power, and wisdom, and love, and thus the soul is like God through this transformation" (C. 39.4). John stresses the same idea again in his last reference to the Trinity: "[T]he soul will participate in God himself by performing in him, in company with him, the work of the Most Blessed Trinity" (C. 39.6).

The Father leads to mutual surrender in love

While John prefers to speak of "God" he does explicitly refer to the Father on five occasions. In the first stanza the soul asks the Father to reveal the essence of the Son, for the Father focuses totally on the Son, "for the Son is the glory of the Father" (C. 1.5). Later, as the bride affirms the presence of the Beloved in multiple manifestations of creation, she acknowledges that there are many mansions in the Father's house (C. 14-15.3). As the bride journeys on, she finds in spiritual marriage that the Father favors her so much that there is a mutual surrender, and "the Father himself becomes subject to her for her exaltation" (C. 27.1). Later, as she longs for the union of eternity, she thanks and loves the Father for having predestined her to this loving union (C. 37.6), in which he loves her with the same love he has for the Son (C. 39.5).

The Son is the Bridegroom, the Lover, and the teacher of love

Only the bridegroom can heal. This commentary of John of the Cross deals "with the exchange of love between the soul and Christ, its Bridegroom" (C. Title). Christ is the Bridegroom, the divine Word whose hiding place is in the bosom of the Father; he is the spouse from the very beginning of the poem, long before we arrive at the description of spiritual marriage (C. 1.1-3). The divinity of the Word, the Bridegroom, is the delight and glory of the Father (C. 1.5), hidden in the bosom of the Father, and also found hidden in the soul. The soul must enter this hiddenness to possess the Bridegroom "through the special grace of divine union with God" (C. 1.11). Then "Remaining hidden with him, you will experience him in hiding, that is, in a way transcending all language and feeling" (C. 1.9). The soul soon discovers that the Bridegroom visits the soul, like a stag, and then quickly leaves (C. 1.15), and the soul feels that only the Beloved can heal these wounds of love (C. 1.20). Already at the outset of the poem we find that the Beloved surrenders to the soul when she surrenders to the Beloved (C. 1.21). In this early phase of purification when the soul encounters God just through intermediaries, the soul discovers that Wisdom, the Son of God, and spouse, is only found when she abandons all forms of self-satisfaction (C. 3.3). All gratifications and satisfactions of a temporary, sensory, and spiritual nature block the direct way to Christ, for they are obstacles to the way of the cross of Christ, the Bridegroom (C. 3.5). As the bride becomes love-sick in the Bridegroom's absences, she learns that only the Bridegroom's presence can heal (C. 6.2). Through contemplation that illumines the world, the lover finds the beauty of the Beloved in the whole world. Illumined with knowledge of God through creation and rational creatures is positive but inadequate and leaves her full of pain, for every revelation highlights the unknown more than the known, for God is indescribable (C. 7.9). The Bridegroom wounds the bride with love but does not carry her off to be his own; rather he remains hidden and all the soul sees is a draft or a sketch of her Beloved, insufficient to satisfy her (C. 12.1).

The Beloved delights in the love of the bride.

During the time of spiritual betrothal, the truths of the Beloved, Christ, are infused through faith while still remaining obscure; but the Bridegroom, the Son of God sends his Holy Spirit to the bride (C. 17.8). At this time the Bridegroom delights in the virtues of the bride. "The soul desires this, not for her own pleasure and glory but because she knows that her Bridegroom delights in this, and it is a preparation and foretelling of the coming of the Son of God to take his delight in her" (C. 17.9). The Son grants and makes the soul aware of her gifts and protects her from any rebellious disturbances that can harm her virtues (C. 18.2). The Bridegroom can enter the inner soul of the bride, but she "must hold the door of her will open to the Bridegroom so he may enter through the complete and true 'yes' of love" (C. 20-21.2). Now the Bridegroom, the Son of God, aids his bride by controlling all negative movements in appetites, powers, passions, and faculties, and he perfects the soul in preparation for union. "Because God vitally transforms the soul into himself, all these faculties, appetites, and movements lose their natural imperfections and are changed to divine" (C. 20-21.4). Thus, the Bridegroom finds so much in the bride that delights him.

The Bridegroom and bride mutually surrender in love.

As the bride enters spiritual marriage she realizes that while she was working hard in search of the Beloved, the Bridegroom was working harder to liberate her and perfect her (C. 22.1). He now rejoices and reveals wonderful secrets as to his consort, especially knowledge of the mysteries of the Incarnation (C. 23.1). She appreciates that it was by the cross that the Son of God redeemed and espoused humanity; the first espousal by Christ was at baptism, and the second is now gradually in the union of perfection (C. 23.6). In this union of mutual surrender the bride is united with the Word, the Son of God and she is overcome with praise for him. In spiritual marriage, the Bridegroom communicates profoundly in mutual love (C. 24.3), and gives her his protection. In this union only two things are necessary which are two aspects of the same spiritual commitment, "attentiveness to God and the continual exercise of love in him" (C. 29.1); nothing else matters. "For a little of this pure love is more precious to God and the soul and more beneficial to the Church, even though it seems one is doing nothing, than all these other works put together" (C. 29.2). This is a form of "holy idleness" (C. 29.4). So, spiritual marriage is an experience of the mutuality of love, and the Bridegroom is captivated by the bride's fidelity and grants the bride total transformation.

The Bridegroom prepares the soul for the vision of God. This transformation into the beauty of God communicates the divine mysteries to the bride, and the Bridegroom enters into these mysteries in her company (C. 37.6). Thus, he grants her profound awareness of the mysteries of God in this beatific transformation. At the same time she knows that the Bridegroom has achieved for her total control of the sensory part so that she is ready for the eternal vision of God (C. 40.1).

The Holy Spirit—the Spirit of love

The Holy Spirit is the source of living faith.

In the prologue to the *Spiritual Canticle* John affirms that the Holy Spirit abides in us and explains to us what we cannot understand, including helping John to expound this poem. The wisdom and experience the Holy Spirit imparts is beyond human ability to explain; many have tried, but "the abundant meanings of the Holy Spirit cannot be caught in words" (C. Prologue.1). In the stage of illumination, the Holy Spirit is the source of living water, living faith that is poured out on the soul who burns ardently for deeper union (C. 12.3). When the bride enters spiritual betrothal the Holy Spirit comes to her to raise her up so that she can receive these gifts. In these visits of the Holy Spirit the soul is carried away violently outside of the body without the body's awareness so that all her feelings are in God (C. 13.6). At this time when the bride wants to move out of her body and the Bridegroom wants her to return to her present state for further purification in view of greater love, it is the Holy Spirit who comes to her in contemplation, as the spirit of love, the refreshing breath of the Father and the Son, proceeding from their wisdom (C. 13.11). Even in spiritual betrothal, the bride suffers from the Bridegroom's absences and often experiences spiritual dryness; in such times the bride invokes the Holy Spirit to dispel her dryness and sustain and increase her love (C. 17.2). The Holy Spirit comes as the spirit of the Bridegroom and awakens her love, controls her appetites and strengthens her will. He discloses the inner wealth of her virtues, thus preparing her for the spiritual marriage that lies ahead; thus, these visits of love prepare the soul as a dwelling place for the Beloved (C. 17.8). The soul greatly desires these visits of the Holy Spirit, for when he comes he abides in the soul and fills it to overflowing with divine communications

(C. 18.6). In fact, he intervenes to effect the spiritual union and speaks to the Father and the Son on behalf of the bride (C. 20-21.2).

The Holy Spirit prepares the bride for spiritual marriage and eternal union.

At the time of spiritual marriage the Bridegroom greatly appreciates the many virtues of the bride, for they are gifts he made to her. It is the Holy Spirit who enables these virtues to flourish (C. 24.6), and at the same time inebriates the soul with the wine of fortified love (C. 25.7), while she also responds with greater love. In spiritual marriage the Spirit of the Bridegroom is infused into this union like a torrent of love (C. 26.1), a situation so ineffable that John says "it will be necessary for the Holy Spirit to take my hand and guide my pen" (C. 26.3). This love has seven stages corresponding to the seven gifts of the Holy Spirit (C. 26.3). It is a spiritual marriage of mutual communication in love in the Holy Spirit (C. 30.1), when the Holy Spirit arouses strong love in the bride to make this flight to God (C. 31.4). As the soul looks forward to the union in eternity, she recognizes the Holy Spirit can supply what is lacking for total transformation. In fact, she now loves through the Holy Spirit in this transformation of love (C. 38.3). When she looks to the ineffable unknown of the afterlife she says it is the "spiration of the Holy Spirit from God to her and from her to God" (C. 39.2). Through this work of the Holy Spirit, God transforms the soul into himself (C. 39.5). It was the Son who merited this transformation for the soul, complete transformation in the Holy Spirit (C. 39.5). It is a flame that consumes but is painless, for it is the love of the Holy Spirit (C. 39.14).

The Soul's Experience of God's Transforming Presence

The soul keeps watch over her heart. The soul must approach these experiences with simplicity of spirit, aware that no one can explain the mysteries of God, and each one will derive profit according to his or her own capacity. Only the pure in heart can understand what John writes (C. Prologue.1-3). The soul will serve God well if she passes beyond the stage of beginners and on through the three stages of the spiritual life (C. Theme.1). The journey begins when the soul becomes aware of her immense indebtedness to God, grateful for the many gifts bestowed on her, and afraid that she may have lost God because of her concern over creatures. She says she does not want sensible devotion, but asks the Father for a revelation of the essence of God (C. 1.5). Her Bridegroom tells her that she must seek God in the very center of her own being which is the innermost secret dwelling of God (C. 1.6). So, the soul hears the challenge to seek God within (C. 1.8), to keep watch over her heart, and then God will reveal the inner mysteries of the divinity (C. 1.10). This means seeking God in faith and love until arriving at the possession of God. "Seek him in faith and love, without desiring to find satisfaction in anything, or delight, or desiring to understand anything other than what you ought to know" (C. 1.11).

The soul seeks God through painful darkness. The journey begins in poverty of spirit as the soul feels a deep pain in the absence of the Beloved so soon after initial communication (C. 1.14). As the soul departs on this journey to God, she also departs from this world and its values and from herself in forgetfulness (C. 1.20). This she can do because of God's love within her. In this journey she lives in constant suffering at the absence of her Beloved (C. 1.21).

This pain and unspeakable torment is a purification and preparation for life with God (C. 1.22), a purification of the three faculties of intellect, memory, and will. In confidence she shows her needs to God knowing God will reply, and then she pursues every way to find her Beloved through her good works and contemplation (C. 3.1). She becomes aware of her need to make a single-minded search for God, a search that will require freedom and fortitude, as she strives through prayer and the cross to free herself from all evils (C. 3.5, 9). This is the soul's time of painful purification.

She seeks the healing illumination of her Beloved. This is also a period of illumination when the more the soul knows God the more she longs for the divine presence (C. 6.2). She now seeks the healing presence of her Beloved and asks for essential knowledge of him for all else is inadequate. "Among all worldly delights and sensible satisfactions and spiritual gratification and sweetness, there is certainly nothing with the power to heal me, nothing to satisfy me" (C. 6.3). So, the soul makes it clear that she does not want any more messengers of God; rather she says "Now wholly surrender yourself" (C. 6.6). Continuing to live with life's limitations becomes profoundly painful (C. 8.2). "[T]he soul lives where she loves more than in the body she animates; for she does not live in the body, but rather gives life to the body and lives through love in the object of her love" (C. 8.3). Life is now centered on God and the heart of the lover is set on loving the Beloved not self (C. 9.5), as she longs for fulfillment and the perfection of love (C. 9.7). The soul asks her Beloved to put an end to her painful longings (C. 10.4) and to reveal the beauty of God, even if it means her death (C. 11.2). She is now living on two horizons of life and the closer she draws in love the greater her pain. "The more the object of her desire comes into sight and the closer it draws, while still being denied her, so much more pain and torment does it cause" (C. 12.9).

The bride suffers for love. As the soul enters spiritual betrothal and draws nearer to God the more she is willing to suffer for love (C. 13.1). She experiences the void of God and cries "withdraw" at the intensity of her experience, but she really does not want the withdrawal but rather the ability to receive the experience outside of her body in the spirit (C. 13.5). These experiences are painful for her but later in spiritual marriage she will receive them in peace and calmness (C. 13.6). At the same time these communications that come in contemplation cause a spirit of love in her, and she delights in giving herself and her virtues to her Beloved (C. 16.1). However, for the perfect enjoyment of God all her senses need to be passive. "When the soul reaches a certain degree of interior union of love, the spiritual faculties are no longer active, and much less the corporeal ones, since the union of love is already wrought and the soul is actuated in love" (C. 16.11). The soul now lives with the "driving force of a fathomless desire for union with God" (C. 17.1), and even when she experiences a lack of consolation in her spiritual life the Spirit enlivens her love and her virtues, even to the extent that others see it (C. 17.7). In fact, both the bride and the Bridegroom mutually delight in the bride's virtues. Still, she feels a prisoner in her own body (C. 18.1), and longs for divine communications only on a spiritual level, with nothing for the lower part. "Since the soul desires the highest and most excellent communications from God, and is unable to receive them in the company of the sensory part, she desires God to bestow them apart from it" (C. 19.1). Now the soul is perfectly conformed to the will of God (C. 20-21.11).

The soul is transformed in a new kind of life. The soul is now ready for spiritual marriage, she has been prepared and is strong enough now to receive the gifts of union, and she can unite her weaknesses to the strength of God (C. 22.6). She has been transformed into her God while both retain their own individuality. Much purification has

been achieved, and she can now "kiss" God without any disturbance (C. 22.7). She drinks of her beloved's own love, rejoices in his love of her and of other people, too (C. 25.1), and she forgets all worldly things as she is informed with supernatural knowledge (C. 26.13). In this union of spiritual marriage the soul is transformed into a new kind of life; she can rejoice that all old things have gone, even though some negative traces will always remain in this life (C. 26.17-18).

The soul's every act is love. The soul now surrenders to her Bridegroom, she feels dissolved in love, and holding nothing back, she experiences mutual surrender (C. 27.2). "The sweet and living knowledge that she says he taught her is mystical theology, the secret knowledge of God that spiritual persons call contemplation. This knowledge is very delightful because it is a knowledge through love" (C. 27.5). Totally united to God's will the soul now can do nothing except love (C. 27.8): "[S]he surrendered herself entirely to the Bridegroom without keeping anything back, she now tells her mode and method of accomplishing this, saying that now she occupies her soul and body, her faculties and all her ability, in nothing other than the service of her Bridegroom" (C. 28.2). Everything about her is now given in the exercise of love, a "holy idleness" that "glories in having lost the world and herself for her Beloved" (C. 29.5); she loses interest in all else. "Anyone truly in love will let all other things go in order to come closer to the loved one" (C. 29.10). She offers all the efforts of her life and especially the virtues of her life that she has acquired and which she recognizes as gifts of her Beloved (C. 30.4); these virtues represent acts of love and gifts of love. They are bound together by fortitude into "solitary and strong love" (C. 31.3), bound together in love of God to whom she gives all credit for her life of virtue (C. 32.1). Now she prays to do all works in the grace of God, and even though she is still aware of her former sins, she asks boldly that God forget all her former ways (C. 33.3). In the enrichment of spiritual marriage she discovers peaceful solitude in her Beloved. "In this solitude, away from all things, the soul is alone with God and he guides, moves, and raises her to divine things" (C. 35.5).

The soul loves God as God loves her. In the final stage of the spiritual journey, the soul yearns for union in eternity. She has no activity other than to surrender to the intimacies of love (C. 36.1). "One thing only is left for her to desire: perfect enjoyment of God in eternal life" (C. 36.2). She asks to rejoice in their love, to become more like the beauty of her Beloved, and to know his innermost secrets. This, too, causes her pain: "The purest suffering brings with it the purest and most intimate knowing, and consequently the purest and highest joy, because it is a knowing from further within" (C. 36.12). So, the bride desires to move to the next life in order to be totally with her Bridegroom, there to understand the mysteries of God, to experience the attributes of God, and to appreciate especially the mystery of the Incarnation (C. 37.1). She gives glory to God for her predestination, enters the mysteries with the Beloved in mutual sharing, and thanks the Father for his gifts. The soul and the Bridegroom now love each other as much as they are loved: "[T]o reach the consummation of the love of God, which she has always been seeking; that is, to love God as purely and perfectly as he loves her in order to repay him by such love" (C. 38.2). While the bride must still wait for eternity for the full union she seeks, "And even though in this state of spiritual marriage we are discussing there is not that perfection of glorious love, there is nonetheless a living and totally ineffable semblance of that perfection" (C. 38.4). In this union of the soul and the Beloved, the soul participates in God and performs the work of the Most Blessed Trinity. The bride feels the Beloved speaking within her, and she unites her voice to his and together they give glory to God (C. 39.9). In contemplation the Bridegroom gives the vision of God to her as part of the consummation of their union (C. 39.14). The bride describes in detail how she is now ready for total union; all evil tendencies subdued, she is filled with spiritual goods (C. 40.1), and she asks for transfer from this world to the next in the union of love (C. 40.7).

CONCLUSION

THE SPIRITUAL CANTICLE AND THE SEARCH FOR UNION IN LOVE

Communion in love

The journey to union in love

"Both are one in the transformation in love" (C. 12.7)

The poem and commentary of the *Spiritual Canticle* form one of the greatest treatises on love in all of spirituality. It presents the spiritual journey as a progressive penetration into the depths of divine love, as a transformation in love, and as a realization that life is more set on love than anything else. God is the Spirit of love who raises us up in love, awakens us to the life of love, and inspires us to love more. God steals our hearts for love, enkindles love within us, moves us to freely love God, and rejoices in the love we show. John speaks about love as the all-embracing aspect of our relationship to God: he speaks of the spirit of love, utterances of love, wisdom of love, detachment of love, darkness of love, friendship of love, and knowledge of love.

Every aspect of life is touched and transformed by love. John describes the love with which God transforms the soul as rigorous, intense, impatient, tender, burning, and ardent. This love is vehement, sweet, delightful, intimate, and lofty. It is fortified, inebriating, supreme, generous, pure, solitary, and interior. It is also savory, strong, mighty, indescribable, glorious, and eventually painless. This love is a festivity, it is mutual, enflames the soul, fills her with fervor, refreshes and renews, and gradually produces likeness with the Lover. What extraordinary vocabulary John uses!

In the early stages of her pursuit of her Lover, the bride says she is wounded with love, longs for love, and seeks her Bridegroom with intense impatient love. She claims to truly love God, to have a lover's heart, to love him above all things, and even to feel she is dying with love. As she pursues a life of love and acts always through love, she gives herself totally in love and longs for the wages of this love. She lives in the condition of love, cries out for more love, and longs for love's completion. She feels refreshed and renewed in love, evidences the excesses of love, and makes a true "yes" of her love for her Bridegroom. As she enters spiritual marriage she longs to become perfect in loving her Bridegroom, and feels moved by love to love more. She is now absorbed in love, transformed in love, employs her entire being in loving, and does everything with love. She wants nothing for herself but desires to become like her Lover, as gradually her love becomes God's love.

These are John's description of the bride's love and further pursuit of love from the breathless rush to love in the early chapters, to the enjoyment of love and desire for more love, to the peaceful completion of love in union. When you read this epic of love, you know there cannot be any appropriate ending to the story except that the two be together in a communion of love in which they give themselves to each other, keeping nothing back. Now the soul's total self-gift reflects God's total self-gift which has always been there drawing the soul throughout the journey.

This communion in love started with spiritual betrothal when the Bridegroom fills his bride with gifts, virtues, knowledge, peace, and the gentleness of his love (C. 14-15.2). The communion of spiritual marriage includes the Bridegroom's revelation of wonderful secrets, "for true and perfect love knows not how to keep anything hidden from the beloved" (C. 23.1). As she enters the inner wine cellar she encounters the intimacy of the Bridegroom's love "which is the union with God, or transformation, through love" (C. 26.2). Then everything leads her to increased love (C. 28.8). Later, when the soul is won over to love, she considers everything else to be of no importance, and in "solitary love" and even in "holy idleness" she focuses exclusively on her "attentiveness of love towards God" (C. 29.3-5).[33]

This communion in love is first of all a time of gratitude and mutual appreciation, as the Bridegroom and bride celebrate the bride's purity, fulfillment of her desires, and all the rewards of her labors, while they also celebrate her contemplation and willingness to leave all in the pursuit of love. John describes something of this mutual celebration in the *Living Flame*: "A reciprocal love is thus actually formed between God and the soul, like the marriage union and surrender, in which the goods of both . . . are possessed by both together" (F. 3.79).This loving transformation leads to intensified love and the bride senses "a spiritual communion of exceedingly agreeable interior love with him" (C. 30.1). The soul acknowledges that all she has comes from God's love. God sees the divine self in her, and he loves in her his own love and makes her his equal (C. 32.6). In the communion of love, "God here is the principal lover, who in the omnipotence of his fathomless love absorbs the soul in himself" (C. 31.2)

In this communion of love the bride longs to receive more love, become like her Beloved, and penetrate the secrets of the divine mysteries (C. 37). She has become new, enriched with virtues—gifts of her Beloved. They are all bound together with strong love, so much so that when he looks at her he sees his own gifts, sees himself. "So great is this union that even though they differ in substance, in glory and appearance the soul seems to be God and God seems to be the soul" (C. 31.1).

This communion in faith and love leads the bride to a total integrated self-gift, and she wants to occupy herself with nothing more than to love. In this communion and refreshment of love, they enjoy each other in solace and satisfaction. This is what the bride has always been seeking, and as she so often felt wounded with love, so now her love wounds her Bridegroom (C. 31.9). This was her goal and she yearns for its completion in eternity, "to reach the consummation of the love of God . . . to love God as purely and perfectly as he loves her in order to repay him by such love . . . to love the Bridegroom as perfectly as he loves her" (C. 38.2). Ultimately this communion in love will include immersion in the life of the Trinity (C. 39.4). The goal is not just union but a union that implies total renewal of self.

A vision of love

"Nothing is obtained from God except by love" (C. 1.13)

John presents us with a wonderful and exciting understanding of the spiritual journey that we are all called to undertake. However, he does more than that; he gives us a vision for life in community, whether ecclesial or civil. He gives us a vision of love for the world. In one of his most famous sayings he reminds us, "When evening comes, you will be examined in love" (S. 60). In his "Romances" he outlined God's strategy of love for the world, and in his poems and major works places before us our vocation to love. This is a hard journey filled with sacrifice, but humanity is not destroyed in this journey but reaches its full potential. Experiencing God's love is a learning situation for us. We learn the importance of love in our experience of God's love for us, see the example of love in God's approach to this world and to ourselves, and know the gift includes a challenge to live the love of faith. In thinking about God, scrutinizing and seeking answers to questions of belief and religion are not enough; we must transform ourselves by love. But God is not known by what we think or by our arguments, no matter how persuasive we may think they are. Rather, we experience God in love, and we know God through lives based on love.

Our experience forces us to take a stand and to live differently because we know we are loved. Our own awareness enables us to glimpse transcendent reality—that it is love that is the basis for life in this world and for life beyond the normal realms of experience. We cannot merely believe in the power of love, we must act on that conviction and show our dedication in action. This means making decisions based on the most loving thing to do. When we live in this way, we ourselves are the first focus of transformation. We change our own attitudes to life, rejecting selfishness, greed, and self-satisfaction, and thus we move away from self-centeredness to self-transcendence. This is a rigorous self-training and eventually leads to the integration of all aspects of life in loving self-gift to God. This single-hearted pursuit of the way of love transforms our decisions, actions, and purposes in life. John's spirituality and vision of humanity is always practical, he focuses on men and women in need of transformation. In the *Spiritual Canticle* he offers us a vision for the world; a vision of love.

Appendix I

REFLECTIONS ON SOME KEY TERMS USED BY JOHN IN THE SPIRITUAL CANTICLE

ARIDITY

Aridity or dryness is part of the purification process one experiences in contemplative prayer. It refers to those times when one experiences no consolation in prayer and no felt experience of God. In this aridity one experiences one's total inability to progress in prayer and realizes that only God's transforming gifts in contemplative prayer can help one move forward. John sees this as one of the three signs that a person is ready to move forward in the spiritual life.

CONFIRMATION IN GRACE

"And thus I think that this state (spiritual marriage) never occurs without the soul's being confirmed in grace, for the faith of both is confirmed when God's faith in the soul is here confirmed" (C. 22.3). A person is always physically free to return to a situation of sin, but following the intense union experienced between the bride and the Bridegroom, their love for each other is so firm that the bride because of the gifts of her Bridegroom is firm in her love for him. So much so that she is confirmed in her situation of grace, and does not make serious sin choices leading her away from God.

CONTEMPLATIVE PRAYER

Contemplative prayer is a gift of God and occurs in the soul when he or she is willing to leave aside meditative and discursive prayer and allows God to take over all the movements of the soul. John identifies three signs that a person is ready for contemplative prayer (A.2. 13; N. 1. 9; F. 32-39). In contemplative prayer the person experiences that God is present, it is an immediate and direct contact with God that includes an intuition that may be intense and profound, or very quiet, simple, and almost imperceptible. This is when a soul is moved passively by God who infuses knowledge and love. This experience is not in words but in love and it is ineffable, indescribable.

The first phase of contemplation is the purification and transformation of prayer from discursive meditation to infused prayer beyond rational processes, a development fostered by God within a person who is willing to let go of previous forms of meditation or discursive prayer in his or her relationship with God. The second phase of contemplation is the purification and transformation of one's ways of knowing, remembering, and loving God. So this second phase transforms what we know of God by purifying our three spiritual faculties of intellect, memory, and will.

DARK NIGHT

John seldom refers to the dark night and darkness in the *Spiritual Canticle*, preferring "The tranquil night at the time of the rising dawn" (C. 14-15.22-23). It refers to the purification and transition from beginners to proficients, and later in the spiritual journey from proficient to perfect. While John does not use this imagery in the *Spiritual Canticle* he still highlights the two periods of purification (stanzas 1-5) and illumination (stanzas 6-12). The experience of darkness and pain in the *Dark Night* is replaced with painful longings and a sense of abandonment in the *Spiritual Canticle*. In both cases the experience leaves the soul feeling helpless in spiritual growth and totally dependent on God.

DESIRE

When John speaks of desire he is describing an attitude of the whole person, an existential yearning or longing to be who we are called to be, who we need to be in order to find peace and fulfillment in life and who we are called to be in loving union with God. When John speaks of desire he is describing what is at the core of our humanity. The desire he describes is the cry of humanity for fulfillment in the union of love. Desire's original focus is on "your Beloved whom you desire and seek" (C. 1.8). So, the desire John presents is the human heart seeking meaning and fulfillment and finding them in love. It is no use seeking fulfillment in the accumulation of desires outside ourselves (C. 1.8). So, desire is fulfilled in the interior recollection of our own hearts, for our Lover resides within. "Desire him there, adore him there" (C. 1.8) for he whom your soul loves is within you.

Desire by itself is not enough, we must do something about it, we must do all we can to satisfy our desire (C. 3.1). Among the primary means are the uprooting of false loves, the practice of virtues, and the spiritual exercise of active and contemplative life. Everything that is not focused on desire for God is a distraction. Desire is for greater love and union, from early stages of love and excitement in pursuing her Lover, through periods of pain and loss at his absence, and on to spiritual betrothal and marriage (C. 9.7). The soul is filled with impatient love that allows no rest, no delays in the ongoing pursuit of greater love. Desire for deeper love and union is what propels and motivates the soul in her ceaseless pursuit of her Lover.

DIVINE COMMUNICATIONS

God communicates something of the inner wonders of divine life in many ways and through many intermediaries—the beauty of the world, the giftedness of people, the mysteries of the spirit world. John insists: "It is noteworthy that, however elevated God's communications and the experiences of his presence are, and however sublime a person's knowledge of Him may be, these are not God essentially, nor are they comparable to Him because, indeed, He is still hidden to the soul" (C. 1.3). The bride, however, says she wants no more intermediaries but tells the Bridegroom that she wants *direct communication*—give yourself entirely to me, surrender yourself, give me complete possession of you (C. 6.6). In fact, all *natural communication* can be a distraction, and in her "fathomless desire for union with God" she experiences constant disturbance in any other communication (C. 17.1). Rather, she wants *spiritual communication* as when the Beloved vitally communicates the divine attributes, "an unveiling of truths about the divinity and a revelation of His secrets" (c. 14-15.15). The Bridegroom also wants to communicate the divine self in everything. "[T]he Beloved is all these things in Himself, and that He is so also for her, because in such superabundant communication from God, the soul experiences and knows the truth of St. Francis' prayer: "My God and my all" (C. 14-15.5). Later, the bride receives *substantial spiritual communication* (C. 20-21.12) that the Spirit grants "in the faculties and virtues of the soul" (C. 18.6), enabling the bride to control all other disturbances because of the strength she receives in the spiritual communication and self-surrender the Bridegroom makes of himself. As the divine communication becomes more spiritual it is less understandable to the senses.

EXPERIENCE OF UNION

The experience of union confirms everything that the soul believes, longs for, and pursues. In the spiritual journey, God gradually prepares the soul for the experience of union in spiritual marriage when she is strong enough to receive the gifts of union and that can unite her weaknesses to the strength of God (C. 22.6). In this experience of union she is transformed into her God while both retain their own individuality. In this experience of union the soul is transformed into a new kind of life; she can rejoice that all old things have gone even though some negative traces will always remain in this life (C. 26.17-18). In this experience of union the soul surrenders to her Bridegroom, she feels dissolved in love, and holding nothing back experiences mutual surrender (C. 27.2). Everything about her is now given in the exercise of love, a "holy idleness" that "glories in having lost the world and herself for her Beloved" (C. 29.5); she loses interest in all else. Her primary activity is love and its intimacies with God, and all her activities are now in God and within God's love (C. 36.1). In this experience she asks to rejoice in their love, to become more like the beauty of her Beloved, and to know his innermost secrets. This, too, causes her pain, so, the bride desires to move to the next life in order to experience union totally with her Bridegroom, there to understand the mysteries of God, to experience the attributes of God, and to appreciate especially the mystery of the Incarnation (C. 37.1). In this union of the soul and the Beloved, the soul participates in God and performs the work of the Most Blessed Trinity. In contemplation the Bridegroom gives the vision of God to her as part of the consummation of their union (C. 39.14). The bride describes in detail how she is now ready for total union; all evil tendencies subdued, she is filled with spiritual goods (C. 40.1), and she asks for transfer from this world to the next, there to experience the union of love (C. 40.7).

GOD'S BEAUTY

John tells us that we experience the ineffable revelation of God in contemplative experiences in which our prior inadequate experiences of God are replaced by vital experiences of the attributes of God. John uses all the traditional attributes of God to describe divine life, but he adds one which is original to him, even though used by other mystics since that time. He uses the word beauty to describe God, always using the noun form (hermosura) rather than the adjective. This unusual description is not used analogically from the beauty of nature, but rather is clearly intended to refer to the inner being of God. This is a vision of the essence of God—*essential vision*. He describes the seeker in the *Spiritual Canticle* deliberately asking God "to show her his beauty, his divine essence" (C. 11.2), so that the person may be granted "a certain spiritual feeling of his presence" and some deep glimpses of his divinity and beauty (C. 11.1). So, for John beauty is a divine attribute equal to the divine essence itself.

ILLUMINATION

The illuminative way is that period in the spiritual journey when beginners leave aside their immature ways of relating to God and become proficients. It marks the transition from meditation and discursive prayer to infused recollection. It is a passive experience, meaning it is a time when God illumines the soul more deeply about who God is and how God acts. John describes this stage in the spiritual life in stanzas 6-12 of the *Spiritual Canticle*. Having passed through trials of longings and sufferings, bitterness, mortification, and meditation in the period of purgation of beginners, in stanza 6 the soul enters contemplation and realizes that it is God who draws her to an appreciation of the divine life. In the earlier stanzas the bride struggles to move to God in love, now God becomes her teacher, transforming her through the illumination of contemplation. This is a painful period, with similarities to the dark night. It is painful, like a wound, a deep sore, and even death—all part of impatient love (C. 7.2-4). "The more the object of her desire comes into sight and the closer it draws, while being denied her, so much more pain and torment does it cause" (C. 12.9). Having received this illumination, the soul longs for union.

PRESENCE OF GOD

John reminds us that God is present to us in one of three ways (C. 11.3). God is present to all creatures by giving them and sustaining them in life and being—this is the *presence by essence*. All beings have this. Then, God is present by abiding in the soul who is without serious sin—not all have this *presence by grace*. God also "grants his spiritual presence to devout souls in many ways by which he refreshes, delights, and gladdens them" (C.11.3)—*presence by spiritual affection*. Yet, each of these is still inadequate, for God remains hidden and does not reveal the divine essence. All quality presence is a presence of participation and love. Thus, the relationship between members of the Trinity consists in the love that unites them. The presence of God is always a *presence of love*. We know God by means of the divine attributes that describe essential characteristics of God (F. 3.2). This is not an intellectual exercise, for the bride will enjoy "the fruition and delight of the love of God overflowing from knowledge of his attributes" (C. 37.8). The attribute that John favors is "beauty" and at the end of the journey of love the bride proclaims, "Let us rejoice, Beloved, and let us go forth to behold ourselves in your beauty" (C. stanza 36). Here she enjoys the *essential presence* of her Beloved for beauty is equal to the divine essence (C. 11.2). In this presence which she has sought, she is inebriated in the love of God, transformed through divine love, and rejoices gratefully in the love she receives.

PRIMITIVE RULE/PRIMITIVE OBSERVANCE

While this is not used in the *Spiritual Canticle* it is used in the text and it is useful to clarify it.

When we read that John wished to return to the primitive observance, it does not mean returning to the original rule as given to the monks on Mount Carmel by Albert, Patriarch of Jerusalem. It simply means returning to the Rule as it was practiced before a series of adaptations that some considered a weakening of the force of the rule. In the case of the Carmelites, first nuns and then friars, reform meant going back to the primitive observance and laying aside all the dispensations granted by popes from Eugene IV (1432) onward, and partly as a result of problems caused by decline, the Hundred Years War, schism, abuses in the mendicant orders, and the Black Death. The mitigations were considered a softening of the original vocation, and reform demanded they be laid aside. When Teresa invited John and his first companion, Antonio de Herédia, to join the reform, it essentially meant a return to simplicity, authenticity of Religious life, austerity, poverty, deeper silence and solitude to allow for contemplation.

SPIRITUAL BETROTHAL

Spiritual betrothal, or espousal, or engagement is described by John in stanzas 13-21 of the *Spiritual Canticle*. The period of spiritual betrothal is an in-breaking of God's transforming love in the soul and includes special communication of God's loving presence. The person feels protected from previous disturbances, but also feels the pain of the absence of the Lover. These pains are intense and have similarities with the night of spirit in the *Dark Night*. One now sees one's own gifts, longs for transformation of spiritual faculties, and yearns for the deeper union of the next stage—spiritual marriage.

SPIRITUAL FACULTIES

The three spiritual faculties are intellect, memory, and will. One of the most important components of a person's transformation into what he or she is called to be is God's impact on life by means of the three theological virtues. By re-directing intellect, memory, and will to their God-directed objects of faith, hope, and love, God enables a person to reach his or her full potential (see N.2. 4.2). The intellect should not get bogged down in objects of knowledge or information especially about God, but rather should focus on the knowledge of God which is faith. The memory wastes its energy and consciousness for the present thinking of past gifts or diminishments and the feelings and influences attached to them when the real object of one's yearnings should be the hope of union with God. The will can disperse its energy so easily on multiple objects of desire, but reaches its God-given power when totally integrated in one unified act of love of all that is of and in God. These three powers of the human spirit are what make us who we are.

SPIRITUAL MARRIAGE

Several religious traditions have used marriage to describe the profound union of believers with God, no one more than Teresa of Avila and John of the Cross. John says: "This spiritual marriage is incomparably greater than the spiritual betrothal, for it is a total transformation in the Beloved, in which each surrenders the entire possession of self to the other with a certain consummation of the union of love. The soul thereby becomes divine, God through participation, insofar as is possible in this life" (C. 22.3).

SPOUSAL LOVE

The use of spousal and erotic imagery to describe the union of the soul with God has been part of Christian traditions since the earliest times—Scripture, the Fathers of the Church, Medieval theologians, and especially Teresa of Avila and John of the Cross. The intimate relationship of men and women in falling in love, longing for union, passionate embrace, and human erotic love are seen as the image or metaphor for spiritual union with God, and this relationship becomes a way of expressing our understanding of God's relationship to us. The *Spiritual Canticle* is the story of a young woman who seeks the love of her life and pursues him until she finds him. This is also seen allegorically as the story of our journey to God; seeking, longing, mutual sharing, engagement, marriage, and union.

TRANSCENDENT VALUES

We are people transformed by faith, and the most immediate consequence of faith is our conviction that there is more in life than meets the eye; there is a world that is not immediately apparent. The word "transcendent" means "going beyond" and focuses on those values that are beyond our normal grasp and understanding. Our experience of faith teaches us that there are two horizons to life, and they are intimately linked. We discover in ourselves a center that naturally yearns for transcendent reality, and we live at this level of mystery, where we are enthralled by enduring truths. Everything we think and do is transformed by this awareness of a relationship between our everyday life and a realm of life that gives meaning to this one. "I no longer live within myself and I cannot live without God, for having neither him nor myself what will life be? It will be a thousand deaths, longing for my true life and dying because I do not die" (Stanzas of the soul that suffers with longing to see God, v. 1). Again, here, life is judged and given a new meaning by a horizon of life beyond this one. The *Spiritual Canticle* presumes these two levels of life. In fact, it is the story of the encounter of these to horizons of life—the bride in this world and the Bridegroom coming from a level of life beyond this one and giving meaning to this one.

TRANSFORMATION

From the first pages of the *Spiritual Canticle*, the goal of the journey is clear. "He will bring her to . . . transformation in him through love" (C. 1.10). Transformation takes place in spiritual marriage (C. 23-25) for which all the rest of the *Spiritual Canticle* is a preparation (asceticism (C. 1-5), illumination (C. 6-12), and spiritual betrothal (C. 13-21)). It then continues in eternity through deeper union and the revelation of the divine mysteries (C. 36-40). Transformation takes place in contemplation when we become receptive to God's activity within us, as God purifies our false desires and false gods and fills us with an inflow of divine love. We never earn or achieve transformation, but what we can do is endeavor with God's grace to conform our will to the divine. It starts with God's self-gift, and we then respond by changing our lives and developing virtues. Although it is a gift, we can ready ourselves to receive this God-given transformation. The goal of the spiritual journey is transformation of the bride into becoming the Bridegroom's true lover. This implies removing false loves, controlling all faculties, focusing everything on the Beloved, and becoming more and more like him in love.

In the transformation of spiritual marriage the bride possesses her Lover and is possessed by him. The union is so intimate that both appear to be God. In this *transforming union*, the Bridegroom transforms his bride by endowing her with gifts and virtues, giving her union, perfect love, and spiritual peace. He establishes mutuality in love, protects her from all threats, grants her habitual tranquility, and makes her equal to him in love—thus in this *transforming love* she enjoys a union of likeness with her Beloved (C. 24). The bride thus transformed in the intimacy of love enjoys these gifts in the very depths of her being. This union leads her to forgetfulness and withdrawal from all that is not conducive to this intimate love and control of all desires and pleasures in anything other than God. Now, all is enjoyed in God.

UNION

There is a union that all creatures enjoy because God is present to them, maintaining them in existence. This is an *essential union* or *natural union*. The goal of the spiritual journey is *supernatural union*. Thus the bride undertakes her spiritual journey because she longs to be united with her Beloved through the union of love, insofar as this is possible in this life (C. 1.4). This union—a union of likeness—that she seeks results from her total dedication to God (C. 12.7-8). At the time of spiritual espousal the bride enjoys a union of love which is bestowed on her by God in contemplation—*contemplative union* (C. 14-15.2). This *supernatural union* results from the conformity of the bride's will with God's, part of her transformation in God, and participation in the life of God. "When a soul reaches a certain degree of *interior union of love*, the spiritual faculties are no longer active, much less the corporal ones, since the union of love is already wrought and the soul is actuated in love" (C. 16.11). As a result of this total conformity of the spiritual faculties (intellect, memory, and will) the soul is in *actual union* which is a *transitory union*. The situation changes in spiritual marriage when the bride surrenders herself completely to her Beloved in a *union of likeness*. Spiritual marriage is the consummation of the union of love—each surrenders his or her entire self to the other (C. 22.3). However, it is God who causes the purity and perfection necessary for this surrender and resulting union. This is the union of two wills in fidelity and stability (C. 27.6). All three faculties are affected by this union (C. 26.6-9) that is now *habitual union* or *permanent union* or *substantial union* for the soul is now in permanent union with God in the very substance of the soul—it is a *state of union*. One's total life is now given entirely to God. In the union of love all the spiritual faculties are dedicated and devoted to God's service, as are all natural abilities (4 passions, the natural appetites, and other energies). In fact, every act is now love (C. 28.8). John also refers to union in the next life, *union of glory* or *total union*.

WOUNDS OF LOVE

John uses the term "wound of love" twenty times in the *Spiritual Canticle*. Generally, it describes the pain the bride experiences in her unfulfilled longings to be with her Lover. She sees traces of him in the beauty around her (C. 6.1), in the knowledge of God she receives through the mediation of irrational creatures, and in the higher knowledge she receives through rational creatures (C. 7.1). The pain the bride experiences in the absence of her Lover is sometimes just a wound, often a sore wound, and sometimes even the festered wound even to an experience of death (C. 7. 2-4). Throughout the *Spiritual Canticle* the wounds of love result from a gift of the Beloved that instead of satisfying leaves her in greater pain at her sense of her Beloved's absence and her own increasing desire to be with him in union. The more she experiences and reflects on these partial presences of her Beloved, the more she feels wounded with love. "For all of them leave you wounded with vehement love" (C. 8.2).

Being wounded with love is not just an experience of the bride (C. 13.9). The Lover too is wounded with his bride's love (C. 35.7), with the purity of her faith (C. 31.9), and with her willingness to wait in solitude (C. 35.7). Both the bride and the Bridegroom long to be with each other and are in pain until that union is complete.

NOTES

1. I am presuming that readers already know the major phases of the life and ministry of John of the Cross. Here I just present the basic outline. A more detailed presentation can be found in my previous books, *The Contemporary Challenge of John of the Cross*, and *The Dark Night is our Only Light.* See also Ruiz Salvador, Frederico and others. *God Speaks in the Night*. Washington , DC: ICS Publications, 1991. For the most detailed life of John readers can consult Fr Crisogono de Jésus Sacramentado, *The Life of St. John of the Cross* (New York: Harper and Brothers, 1958), and Fr Bruno de Jésus-Marie, *St. John of the Cross* (New York: Sheed and Ward, 1932).

2. Xavier Pikaza, "Amore de Dios y contemplación crisitana: Introducción a San Juan de la Cruz." *Actas III*, p. 53.

3. Colin Thompson, *St. John of the Cross: Songs in the Night* (Washington, DC: Catholic University Press of America, 2003), p. 55.

4. Stanzas 1-31 – Prison in Toledo (1577-1578); stanzas 32-34 Baeza (1578); stanzas 35-39 Granada (1582); and stanza 11- unknown when added. There are some differences among the witnesses. Magdalena del Espíritu Santo thought John composed the last ten stanzas in Baeza (1579-82). Francisco de la Madre de Dios reported that John asked her about her prayer, and when she said she just looks at the beauty of God, he went into ecstasy and wrote 5 verses on beauty.

5. Fr. Crisogono, pp. 222-223, points out: "His major works, then, were a gradual development. They were preceded by small fragments which developed into chapters. It should be remarked, however, that these first writings already have a definite character about them."

6. The most reliable manuscript of the *Spiritual Canticle* is Codex Sanlúcar de Barrameda, a copy with personal notes and corrections by John, and this serves as a bridge from the original to this early copy. Several other copies also contain corrections and editing by John.

7. John's works were first published by P. Salabanca in 1618, but without the *Spiritual Canticle* because it was similar to the *Song of Songs*, and the latter was not advisable in times of fear of Illuminism and the threat of censure by the Inquisition.

8. There are 20 early copies of A with 39 stanzas and 11 copies of B with 40 stanzas (including the addition of stanza 11). This is an interesting verification of both redactions.

9. It is generally thought that John composed 31 stanzas in prison. Magdalena del Espíritu Santo said she saw up to the stanza that begins "you girls of Judea," which at the time could have been stanza 31. It is now stanza 18, and we are really not sure what the order was when John came out of prison.

10. Some authors express disappointment at the detailed commentary, suggesting John could not possibly have had this in mind when he wrote the poem. The commentary gives the impression that every word is packed with detailed allegorical meanings, some quite far-fetched. See for example Gerard Brenan, St *John of the Cross: His Life and Poetry* (Cambridge, England: Cambridge University Press, 1973), pp. 121-122.

11. John told Sr. Ana de San Alberto that he repeated the poems often and consigned them to memory in view of eventually writing them down.

12. Fr. Federico Ruiz Salvador suggests a different outline which has its own logic and attraction (see *Introducción a San Juan de la Cruz*, (Madrid: Biblioteca de Autores Cristianos, 1968), p. 226. 1. Stanzas 1-11: Search for the Beloved. 2. Stanzas 12-16: Meeting of the lovers. 3. Stanzas 17-26: Mystical union of the spouses. 4. Stanzas 27-31: Spiritual matrimony. 5. Stanzas 32-34: Life of intimacy in spiritual matrimony. 6. Stanzas 35-39: Desire for glory

13. Arthur Symons, "The Poetry of Santa Teresa and San Juan de la Cruz," *The Contemporary Review*, 75 (1899): 546.

14. Magdalena del Espíritu Santo once asked John if God had given him the words of the poems, to which he replied, "Daughter, sometimes God gave them to me and sometimes I found them myself."

15. John is immersed in Scripture and has a feel for its message. He thinks of the biblical writers as great figures who write as a result of their own spiritual experiences. He also uses a lot of biblical archetypes: Moses—hiding in the cleft of the rock (C. 10. 1), Exodus—liberation from slavery C. 11.5), Noah—the image of the returning dove (C. 34. 4), Noah's ark—the Father's many mansions (C. 14-15.3), Elijah—the

gentle breeze (C. 14-15.14), Bride—from the *Song of Songs*. He also has many references to the Psalms, to Job, and to St. Paul.

16. John had read a book by Sebastián de Cordoba, *Love of God for the Soul*, published in 1575, in which the author takes Garcilasco and transfers much of it into religious verse.

17. See Brenan, *St John of the Cross: His Life and Poetry*, pp. 113-115, where he develops this idea of "fusion."

18. The order of the verses does not seem to be a watertight arrangement; John of course changed the order. Edith Stein suggested that John sang unconnected verses to himself with no particular order.

19. Allison Peers, *General Introduction to the Ascent of Mount Carmel* (New York: Doubleday and Co., Image Books, 3rd rev. ed. 1958), p. 51

20. Gerard Brenan, *The Literature of the Spanish People* (Penguin: Harmondsworth, 1963), p. 156.

21. Thompson, p. 14.

22. See a more detailed description of the environment in which John wrote in my book, *The Dark Night is Our Only Light*, chapter two.

23. Edith Stein, commenting on the fact that quotes from Scripture are not as readily appropriate and understandable in the *Spiritual Canticle* as in the *Living Flame* says: "They often give the impression of wanting to prove that certain daring expressions are based on Scriptural usage and employed in the same sense." See *The Science of the Cross: A Study of St. John of the Cross* (London: Burns and Oates, 1960), p. 178.

24. See Antonio T. de Nicolás, *St. John of the Cross: Alchemist of the Soul* (New York: Paragon House, 1989), pp. 5-6.

25. Thompson, pp. 150-152, points out that some of John's interpretations seem strange to modern mindsets: 1. John takes for granted things we do not; for example the traditional approach to the *Song of Songs*. 2. John saw connections where we do not, for example in Scripture. 3. John had an allegorical frame of mind which is unusual for us. 4. John saw several layers of meaning in the same text, for example for soul, the Church, and the world. 5. John presumed the insufficiency of language.

26. Ross Collings, *John of the Cross* (Collegeville, MN: Liturgical Press, 1990), p. 19. "[N]o one is excluded from this world of grace mediated by St. John. His writings do not belong to a close circle of mystical initiates; every Christian—indeed, every human person—can rightly understand himself to be in some way 'the soul' on the way to union of love with God. The mystical intensity does not narrow the way, but rather gives it a universal and cosmic scope."

27. Brenan, *St John of the Cross: His Life and Poetry*, p. 122.

28. Stein, p. 181.

29. In all key concepts in the *Spiritual Canticle* both the Bridegroom and bride are directly involved together. Here, simply for easier organization I have divided the key concepts into two groups; those concepts that more directly concern God and those that refer a little more to the bride. It is not a theological or spiritual division but rather one to help easier reading. I have thus divided the material into two chapters.

30. John Welch, *When Gods Die: An Introduction to John of the Cross* (New York/Mahwah: Paulist Press, 1990), p. 157.

31. Symons, p. 546.

32. Thompson, p. 277.

33. For Teresa the state of union is a prelude to intense activity, whereas in John it seems to supplant activity.

BIBLIOGRAPHY

Brenan, Gerald. *The Literature of the Spanish People*. Penguin:
Harmondsworth, 1963.

Brenan, Gerald. *St John of the Cross: His Life and Poetry*.
Cambridge, England: Cambridge University Press, 1973.

Brenan, Gerald. *The Literature of the Spanish People*.
Harmondsworth: Penguin, 1963.

Bruno de Jésus-Marie. *St. John of the Cross*. New York: Sheed and
Ward, 1932.

Collings, Ross. *John of the Cross*. Collegeville, MN: Liturgical
Press, 1990.

de Cordoba, Sebastián. *Love of God for the Soul*. 1575.

Crisogono de Jésus Sacramentado, *The Life of St. John of the
Cross*. New York: Harper and Brothers, 1958.

Doohan, Leonard. *The Contemporary Challenge of John of the
Cross*. Washington, DC: ICS Publications, 1995.

Doohan, Leonard. *The Dark Night is our Only Light: A study of the
book of the Dark Night by John of the Cross*. 2013.

Doohan Leonard. *John of the Cross: Your spiritual guide*. 2013.

de Nicolás, Antonio T. *St. John of the Cross: Alchemist of the Soul*.
New York: Paragon House, 1989.

Peers, E. Allison. *General Introduction to the Ascent of Mount
Carmel*. (New York: Doubleday and Co., Image Books, 3rd
rev. ed. 1958).

Pikaza, Xavier. "Amore de Dios y contemplación crisitana: Introducción a San Juan de la Cruz." *Actas III*. 51-96.

Ruiz Salvador, Federico. *Introducción a San Juan de la Cruz*. Madrid: Biblioteca de Autores Cristianos, 1968.

Ruiz Salvador, Federico and others. *God Speaks in the Night*. Washington , DC: ICS Publications, 1991.

Stein, Edith. *The Science of the Cross: A Study of St. John of the Cross*. London: Burns and Oates, 1960.

Symons, Arthur. "The Poetry of Santa Teresa and San Juan de la Cruz," *The Contemporary Review*, 75 (1899): 542-551.

Thompson, Colin. *St. John of the Cross: Songs in the Night*. Washington, DC: Catholic University Press of America, 2003.

Welch, John. *When Gods Die: An Introduction to John of the Cross*. New York/Mahwah: Paulist Press, 1990.

BOOKS AND E-BOOKS

THE CONTEMPORARY CHALLENGE OF JOHN OF THE CROSS

STUDIES OF THE MAJOR WORKS OF JOHN OF THE CROSS

This series presents introductions to each of the great works of John of the Cross. Each volume is a study guide to one of John's the major works and gives all the necessary background for anyone who wishes to approach this great spiritual writer with appropriate preparation in order to reap the benefits of one of the most challenging figures in the history of spirituality. Each book is a complete introduction offering background, history, knowledge, insight, and theological and spiritual analysis for anyone who wishes to immerse himself or herself into the spiritual vision of John of the Cross..

While targeted to the general reader these volumes would be helpful to anyone who is interested in the spiritual guidance of this saint. These books give insight into the critical components of spiritual life and can be helpful for anyone interested in his or her own spiritual journey. They could be a significant help for the many people involved in the spiritual guidance of others, whether in spiritual direction, retreat work, chaplaincy, and other such ministries. Throughout these books the reader is encouraged to develop the necessary attitudes, enthusiasm, spiritual sensitivity, and contemplative spirit needed to benefit from this spiritual masterpiece of John of the Cross. Attentive reflection on these studies will encourage readers to have a genuine love for John of the Cross and his approach to the spiritual journey.

These books give historical, regional, and religious background rarely found in other introductory books on John of the Cross. They each present an abbreviated and accessible form of John's great works. Later chapters in each book give John's theological and spiritual insights that could be used for personal reflection and group discussion. Sections abound in quotes and references from John's books and each sub-section can be used as the basis for daily meditation. The volumes complement each other, and together give the reader excellent foundation for reading the works of this great spiritual leader and saint.

Volume 1. John of the Cross: Your spiritual guide

This unique book is written as if John of the Cross is speaking directly to the reader. It is a presentation by John of the Cross of seven sessions to a reader who has expressed interest in John's life and teachings. This book introduces the great mystic and his teachings to his reader and to all individuals who yearn for a deeper commitment in their spiritual lives and consider that John could be the person who can guide them.

Table of contents

1. John's life as a contemporary life
2. John as a spiritual guide
3. John's vision of the spiritual life
4. Preparations for the spiritual journey
5. Major moments and decisions in the spiritual life
6. Necessary attitudes during the spiritual journey
7. Celebrating the goal of the spiritual journey

Volume 2. The Dark Night is Our Only Light: A study of the book of the *Dark Night* by John of the Cross

This introduction to the *Dark Night of the Soul* by John of the Cross gives all the necessary background for anyone who wishes to approach this great spiritual work with appropriate preparation in order to reap the benefits of one of the most challenging works in the history of spirituality. The book starts with the life of John of the Cross, identifying the dark nights of his own life. It provides the needed historical, religious, and personal background to appreciate and locate its content. It then presents readers with aids they can use to understand the work. With these preparations in mind the book moves on to present the stages of the spiritual life and the importance of the nights. A summary of John's own work brings readers in direct contact with the challenges of the message and its application today. The book ends with 20 key questions that often arise when someone reads this book.

Table of contents

1. John of the Cross and the dark nights of his own life
2. Influences on John's writing of the *Dark Night*
3. Aids to reading the *Dark Night*
4. Understanding the book of the *Dark Night*
5. The book of the *Dark Night* by John of the Cross – a summary
6. Five key spiritual challenges of the book of the *Dark Night*
7. The dark night in contemporary life
8. Twenty questions for John of the Cross and his book of the *Dark Night*

Volume 3. The *Spiritual Canticle*: The encounter of two lovers. An introduction to the book of the *Spiritual Canticle* by John of the Cross

The book starts with the life of John of the Cross, showing how he was always a model of love in his own life, and how, guided by his own experience he became a teacher of human and divine love and later a poet of human and divine love. The book provides the needed historical, religious, and personal background to appreciate and locate its content. The book then presents the links between John's *Spiritual Canticle* and Scripture's love poem, the *Song of Songs*. A summary of John's own work brings readers in direct contact with the challenges of the message and its application today. With these preparations in mind the book moves on to present the stages of the spiritual life and the importance of the journey of love. The book then focuses on key concepts in the Spiritual Canticle, applying each of them to contemporary situations. Finally it considers the images of God presented in the book and how they relate to the spiritual journey.

Table of contents

Volume 4. *The Living Flame of Love* (Due in 2014).

The *Living Flame of Love* is the final chapter in John's vision of love. It describes the end of a journey that began in longings of love that became an experience of purification for the person seeking union. *The Living Flame of Love* picks up from the final stage of union in the love of spiritual marriage and describes, in great beauty, several aspects of this final stage in the union of love. All these ideas are part of John's wonderful vision of love. Many writers have emphasized the spiritual value of a life of love, but John's vision is more expansive and integrated than approaches presented by anyone else.

Table of contents

1. John's vision of love
2. Preparations for love
3. Introduction to the *Living Flame of Love*
4. The story of the *Living Flame of Love*
5. United in love with the Holy Spirit
6. Immersed in love with the Holy Trinity
7. Transformed by God's love and attributes
8. Understanding the cosmos in union with the love of the Word

ALL BOOKS ARE AVAILABLE FROM AMAZON.COM

ANOTHER BOOK OF INTEREST

The One Thing Necessary: The Transforming Power of Christian Love.

This radical new interpretation of love as the touchstone of the Christian message, explores the human longing for meaning; the Scriptures; the relational model of the Trinity: the ideas of human vocation, destiny and community; the mystical spiritual traditions; and his own experiences to explain what love is, how we find it, and how it can change the world. Each of the seven chapters contains several quotes and focus points at the beginning and provocative questions at the end for reflection or discussion by adult religious educations and bible study groups.

"This book is all about love—and love as the one thing necessary. It is most certainly not about easy love or cheap grace. It is about the transforming power of Christian love. It is not only challenging but disturbing, a book written with conviction and passion."
Fr. Wilfrid Harrington, OP., Biblical scholar.

"[Doohan's] artful gathering and arranging of ideas reminds one of the impact of a gigantic bouquet of mixed flowers chosen individually and with great care." **Carol Blank**, Top 1000 reviewers, USA.

"Would that we heard more about this in our churches and religious discussions because, "this transforming power of Christian love will save the world" (p. 93). **Mary S. Sheridan**, "Spirit and Life."

The One Thing Necessary: The Transforming Power of Christian Love is available from www.actapublications.com and from amazon.com

Readers interested in John of the Cross
can read the author's blog at

johnofthecrosstoday.wordpress.com

and contribute a comment
or become a guest blogger

See the author's webpage at
leonarddoohan.com

40777375R00138

Made in the USA
Lexington, KY
22 April 2015